This is not a recipe book!

For the first time in history (or at least the author's history), there's a yoyo book that is about HOW TO YOYO and not just a book of four dozen trick recipes. Funny thing is this book does have trick recipes in it, 56 in fact (in different levels of detail). Many of these appear nowhere else in print.

The Yonomicon does have everything a beginning yoyoer needs to know in it, but it's written mainly to satisfy the burning question left unanswered by all other yoyo books:

"Okay, now what?"

This is the book for everyone who has bought a yoyo book and learned those tricks. This is the book for anyone who's bought a yoyo book and known all those tricks. This is the yoyo book for anyone who throws a yoyo with a transaxle. This is the yoyo book for anyone who wants to teach those transaxle punks a thing or two about the power of wood. This is the yoyo book for people who don't first think of swimming when someone says, "Freestyling".

The Yonomicon is also the full and complete write up of Quantum Yo Theory, the system for breaking down freestyle string tricks into their most basic units, and TFY Transcription, the way to write it all out. If you think you've seen and thrown it all, Quantum Yo Theory is here to take you in new directions; directions that would scare people who thought the Earth was flat..

Welcome to the New School.

the YONOMICON

an enlightened tome of yoyo tricks

by
Mark
McBride

ISBN: 0-941463-01-X

Printed in the United States of America

10 9 8 7 6 5 4 3 2 1

Nods

Bill M., Kay, Nic, Greg, Steve, Chuck, Mike,
David & Tradd, Bill L., Brian, Todd, Dale, Kevin,
Merlin, Jason, Don, Curtis, John, Chris, Ben,
Mark, Pedro, Duncan & Yomega, the ladies at
Bruckheimer, the blonde from OC, The King,
and The Almighty

Down

SEE HOW THE STRING WINDS ON.... YOU WANT iT TO UNROLL WHEN YOU THROW iT DOWN.

AND YOU WANT AN iNCH OR SO SLACK. iT SMOOTHES OUT YOUR THROW.

1) Turn your hand (the one holding the yoyo) palm up and arm back.

If your yoyo won't come back, but keeps spinning, your string might be loose--a big problem with new strings.

2) Throw it down off the back of your hand, UNROLLING the string.

3) Turn your hand over and when it hits the bottom of the string, give it a little pull.

If your yoyo doesn't go down smooth and dies, you might not be unrolling it. Check your string direction...and check for knots.

Sleeper

1) Throw it down (off the back of your hand, etc.,etc.), **but don't pull it up!**

You can't do this one with a tight string. So keep it loose!

YA GoTTA KNoW ThiS TRiCK! IT'S A BASE FOR A LOT OF OTHERS!

2) Turn your hand over and soften the yo-yo's bottom-**out.** YOU DON'T WANT IT TO BOUNCE AT THE END OF THE STRING.

3)Let it Spin!

4)Give it a little pull.

**TRANSAXLES NEED A BIGGER TUG.

Table of Contents

Introduction

You may have noticed that the first things in this book are two pages on "Down" and "Sleeper" (even before the Table of Contents). These are the two things that you have to know and this book is written assuming that you do. Those two pages are also the very first mock ups of what was later to become The Yonomicon. A year ago I worked (lived) at a yoyo shop in Florida. I used to always say that there were no good yoyo books out there. All of the books on the market were these little piddley things that were great 30 years ago and when you first picked up a yo. But all too quickly I and all the kids who came into the shop and the scene as a whole outgrew them. I said that I'd write a good yoyo book. Those two pages were what I did to show the style to the guy who would later publish it. But being a college kid working on his thesis, I had no time and eventually graduated from college and moved to LA. The book was back burnered and left for cold and congealed.

So a year after I did those two pages, I get a call, "Now is the time for the book." There were all of these little recipe books, as I came to call them, on the shelves and more on the way. This book would pick up where they left off. I was told, "Start at Brain Twister and go from there." The big boy tricks.

Now I was always a fan of string tricks. I didn't do 2 handed stuff or try to loop the thing every way I could; I just wanted to get complex. Knowing that these bigger tricks had parts in common with each other, I figured the best way to explain them would be to break them down into components.

The first thing was mounts. Then came holds. I started getting a stack of index cards with holds on them and figured I had to come up with a system for naming them. And TFY was born. The TFY system and a handy-dandy matrix let me create holds I had never seen but figured out existed (theoretical yoing).

With a firm list of holds, I whipped up a grid and did every move on every hold and figured out what you'd get for each. I wanted an universal map... you'll find it in the last chapter. This book was written three times during the course of writing it.

Take a bunch of math and string and boil it down to a readable goo and then throw in some pictures and a little finesse and let simmer for about 5 months and POOF, The Yonomicon. There's the recipe for a non-recipe yoyo book. Enjoy.

Warning

This book is a headful. It's written to be read through starting at the beginning, but it is a reference book more than anything else. So don't get frustrated. Of course I'm not foolish and I know that just about every kid who buys this is going to skip right to chapter 7 and only then go back to read the rest when they can't figure out the transcribed tricks without pictures. But, trust me, those of you who are patient and disciplined enough to genuinely start at the beginning will get more out of it.

1.
General Knowledge

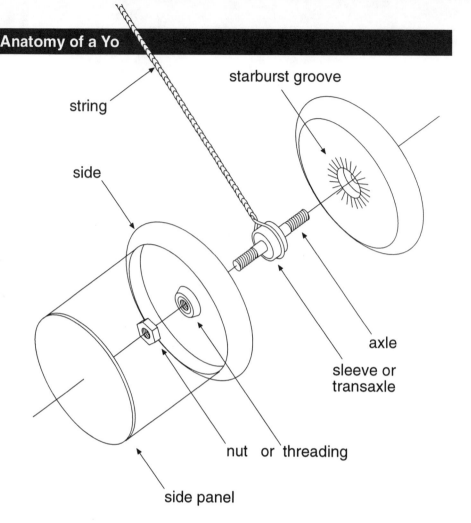

starburst groove

string

side

axle

sleeve or
transaxle

nut or threading

side panel

This is an exploded diagram of a three-piece yo. It's called a three-piece because it's not a one-piece. One-piece yos are made up of 2 sides and an axle, but they can't be taken apart, so they're called "One-piece". "Three-piece" yos are 2 sides and an axle that can be separated.

A few things to watch for in the above diagram: (it's a compilation of designs to give you a feel for the names of parts, not an accurate picture of a particular yo) You'll have either a nut or threading. They do the same thing in the same place so you won't have both. Same with a sleeve or transaxle, you won't have both (see the bit on axles). Side panels are optional, so you may not even have them and a few yos (trans. more often) have a variety of bushings and washers in them. They can be around the axle just about anywhere, so I didn't confuse the diagram by including them. But, watch out for them. And the string gap is the space between the sides where the string goes down to the axle. In this diagram I couldn't really point at it.

Functionally there are 2 kinds of axles, fixed and trans. Fixed axles are axles that are, well, fixed to the yo. They don't spin independently of the sides. The axle spins inside the string with the yo. Transaxles are where string is around a sleeve (the transaxle) that spins around the axle. The string is fixed to the transaxle and the axle spins inside of that. Transaxles are made to have less friction against the axle than the string so you can get longer spins.

Wood is the best material for fixed axles. This isn't just a matter of convenience or tradition (although there is value in tradition); in the late 70's Tom Kuhn, one of the old masters, tested every material he could get his hands on. NASA even sent him samples of stuff and he still came back to wood. I think it has to do with the fibrous make up of wood, but I haven't taken it to the lab.

Since steel is stronger than wood and it's hard to thread a wood pin for unscrewing, a popular design is to have a wood sleeve over a metal bolt. This way you get the advantages of a metal bolt with the string feel of wood.

Transaxles come in a few different varieties. The 2 main varieties are ones that roll and ones that slide. Transaxles that roll are bearings. The string is around the outside of the bearing which rolls on the inside of the bearing that is around the axle. Transaxles that slide are sleeves that are made of a slick material and/or are lubricated so the axle loses its friction by spinning on a slick surface. Since the string is around the transaxle and not around the spinning axle, it's usually best to double loop transaxles (see the string section for details).

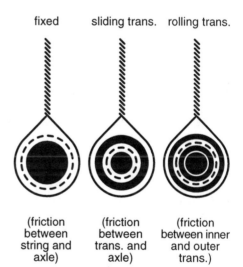

fixed   sliding trans.   rolling trans.

(friction between string and axle)   (friction between trans. and axle)   (friction between inner and outer trans.)

When you pull back a yo, you're putting some slack in the string. With a fixed axle, this allows the string to close up on the axle, thus grabbing it and bringing the yo up. With a transaxle, putting slack in the string allows the friction of the sides to wrap the string around the axle, which then catches and the yo comes up. This means that transaxles need a bigger pull to put more slack in the string to get a return. Fixed axles need less pull and less spin to get a return.

Shape

Yos come in as many different shapes and sizes as you can count. And each shape is going to have its own feel. Which one is best is up to you. The two factors of shape that have the most effect on the performance of the yo are its silhouette and weight distribution. Silhouette is just a fancy way of saying, "the outside shape."

traditional   midline   butterfly

There are three main silhouettes: traditional, midline and butterfly. The big difference is the width of the string gap. A wide gap gives you more room to get the string in there, making it easier to do string tricks. The butterfly shape has the widest string gap and is thus easiest to get on the string for string tricks.

The traditional shape has the narrowest string gap and is better for looping. This has to do with the point where the string bends out of the string gap and it's relationship to centers of gravity and stuff like that. The midline shape is a compromise between traditional and butterfly.

Another factor is weight distribution, where your yo is heavy; what matters is how far out from the axle (center) most of the weight is. The further out, the more leverage you have with your spin so the more efficiently it keeps its plane. This is good for string tricks, but for looping, it's a matter of taste. Edge-heavy designs and weight rings are made to put as much of the weight away from the center as possible.

edge-heavy   hollow   solid

Another factor not to be overlooked is how a shape feels in your hand. This is a matter of personal taste, although I don't know anyone who likes the feel of cornered or sharp edges hitting their hand every time the yo comes back.

The first thing to realize about yo string is that although it looks like 2 strands twisted together into one string (like normal twine), it is not. It is actually one strand folded over and twisted on itself. The folded over end is the end that goes around the axle of the yo.

The first thing to do when you get a new yo (or replace a string) is to adjust the length. Strings will usually come in 3 foot lengths, which is too long for anyone under 5 feet tall. A good rule of thumb is that your string should go from your ankle to your navel. If your string is too long you have to keep your arm up when you throw to keep the yo from hitting the ground and this causes you to lose power in your throw.

It's a good thing to experiment with different string lengths and find one that you like. Shorter strings move faster, but longer strings give you more room. And there are many other variables, you'll just have to experiment. Realize that an inch can make a huge difference so don't be too generous with your adjustments.

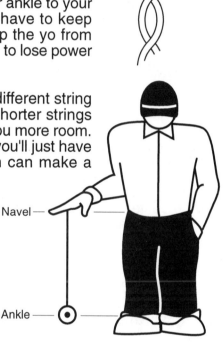

Navel

Ankle

Once you've figured out the length you need, fold over the string about an inch above the height you like. Tie the folded section in a knot. Then cut off the extra end and you'll have the string length you want.

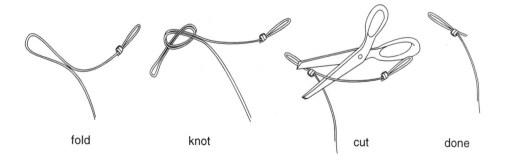

fold   knot   cut   done

The loop you get is not where you put your finger. You put the string through that loop to get a slip knot, and that loop is where you put your finger.

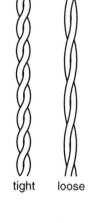

Where you put that knot on your finger is another matter of taste. I , myself, prefer the base knuckle of my middle finger. I do recommend putting the string on your base knuckle if you're planning on doing the high end string moves. It gives you more finger space to work with. And the middle finger is good because it leaves your index finger open on one side and is in a straighter line with your arm for throws. But again, this is all personal opinion. The best choice for you is what feels right. And, that will have a bigger effect on how well you throw than where you have space on your hand.

The next thing to realize about string is that it's twisted and this matters, especially with fixed axles. The tighter your string is twisted the tighter it holds onto the axle. For a fixed axle this means the less it sleeps. When the string is loose, it's grip on the axle is loose and it sleeps easier. So to sleep a fixed axle keep your string loose. To do loop tricks keep it tight.

To tighten the string let your yo die and then spin it to the right (clockwise if you're looking down on it). To loosen it, spin it to the left (counterclockwise). Easy to remember, it's just like a screw: righty-tighty, lefty-loosey.

Now the string is going to tighten or loosen when you're just yoing. Whenever you throw a yo and turn your hand over to get it coming

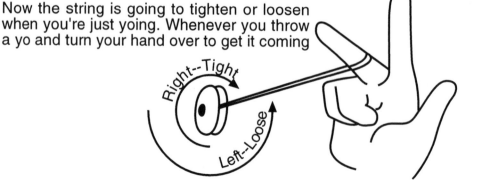

back, you add a half turn to the string. If you're throwing with your right hand this turn is to the right and will tighten the string. If you're on your left hand this will loosen the string. And when you're doing loops it's going to be the opposite. So every so often you need to take the string off your finger and let it dangle. When you take the tension off of the string it will even itself out. You can also do it yourself by killing and spinning the yo or throwing a flying saucer (see that write up for details).

How tight a string is doesn't affect transaxles until it gets to the extreme. If your string gets really tight it will try to coil up and that will mess you up when you're doing a trick. If the string gets too loose, it can start affecting how well it catches. So it's a good idea to keep your string around a normal tension even if you're throwing a transaxle.

Any good yo will out last a cotton string and when that happens it's time to put on a new string. To get the old string off you can either simply untwist it until it gets loose enough that you can pull the yo out or, if you're strong enough, you can just jerk it hard enough to break it at the bottom. Untwisting is usually less painful.

To put the new string on, first pinch it at the bottom and at about 4 inches up. Then untwist this section. When you can, get your fingers in between the strands and open it enough so that you can slide your yo in like a button.

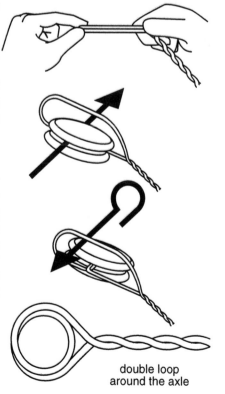

For a single loop, that's it. Slide it on, let the string drop so it tightens up, and wind it. For a double loop, put it through like a single loop then turn it over and put it back through so there's an extra wrap around the axle. Then let the string go and wind it.

You'll want to use a single loop for fixed axles and a double loop for transaxles. The difference is that double loops don't let go of the axle (or transaxle). For a fixed axle this means a double loop won't sleep. For a transaxle this means a double loop will be more reliable and come back up.

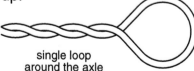

single loop
around the axle

double loop
around the axle

As a quick reminder message, I'll say make sure you start with a tight wound yo and make sure that the yo will be unrolling when you throw it. Curl your arm and then throw the yo down. When it gets to the bottom of the string, turn your hand over and pull it back up.

Right   Wrong

That out of the way, I'll point out that the secret to getting really good spins is to use more than just your wrist (a common mistake). Start with your yo over your shoulder. This way you can use the muscles that move your shoulder (Latissus Dorsi), your elbow (triceps), and your wrist (extender muscles). This will give you much more power because there are more muscles working and your Latissus Dorsi and triceps are much larger muscles.

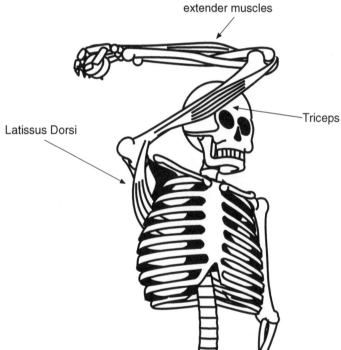

extender muscles

Latissus Dorsi

Triceps

A common mistake is to turn your hand over too early, as in before your yo is out. This will give you slanted throw. Again, don't turn your hand over until the yo has completely left it. If you don't have a straight release, you won't have a straight throw.

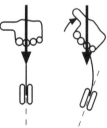

As the old skater mantra says, "If you don't eat asphalt, you aren't trying hard enough tricks." Inevitably, the yo will die. And when it does you have to wind up the string to reset it. To do this you have to either wrap the string around the yo or jump start the spin.

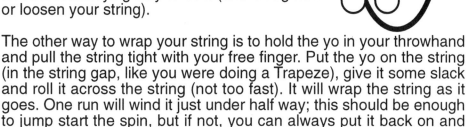

The easiest way to wrap the string is to simply wrap the string with your hand. If you have a transaxle or a really loose string and it won't wrap, simply put your finger tip in the string gap for a few wraps and then let go and continue wrapping. Anyone can do this, but it's the slowest and most annoying way to do it (and it'll tighten or loosen your string).

The other way to wrap your string is to hold the yo in your throwhand and pull the string tight with your free finger. Put the yo on the string (in the string gap, like you were doing a Trapeze), give it some slack and roll it across the string (not too fast). It will wrap the string as it goes. One run will wind it just under half way; this should be enough to jump start the spin, but if not, you can always put it back on and roll it again.

The other method is to jump start the spin. That is getting the spin started with your hand and getting it wrapped like you were just pulling it back up. There are a few ways to do this. The least complicated is to ramp it off your freehand. Basically put the string between index and middle fingers of that hand, pull the string up while you run your hand down the yo giving it some spin. The danger in doing this is that pulling on the string stresses it and wears it out string faster. So make sure you're spinning it and not just tugging on the string.

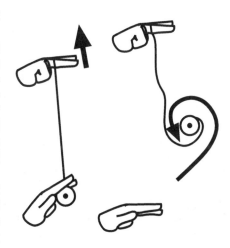

The first bit of science is a vocabulary word: plane. A plane is flat space. Picture an air hockey table. The puck is sliding around on the smooth, flat table top. The table top is a plane. As long as the puck doesn't fly off the table, it's on a plane. It can move around forward and backward and left and right, but there's no up and down. Now let's take that same airhockey puck and put it against a nice flat window. We can slide it all around against the window and as long as you keep it pressed against the window, it will be on a plane. This plane is the window. It's flat, there's up and down and left and right but no forward and backward.

Now a window is physical, you can touch it. And an air hockey table is physical too, but the plane that the yo moves around on is not physical. It's called abstract; it's real, but you can't touch it. When you're yoing, you want to keep your yo on a plane. Imagine you're at the window sliding your hockey puck around on it, staying on that plane. Then someone raises the window. Even if the window isn't there, you know where the plane is because you know where the window was. If you hold the puck and continue to move it around like the window was there, not moving it forward (which would be through the window if it was still there) or backwards (which would pull it off the window if it was still there), then you're keeping the plane.

Keeping the plane is very important in freestyle action. If the yo and the string aren't on the same plane then getting the yo on the string becomes nearly impossible.

The plane of the yo comes from the yo itself. When a yo is spinning it has what is called gyroscopic stability. Gyroscopic stability is the way a yo stays in line and holds an angle when it's spinning. For a quick demonstration, throw a sleeper, then swing it from side to side. Notice how the yo always faces forward and stays at the angle you throw it at, it won't turn or tilt until it runs out of spin.

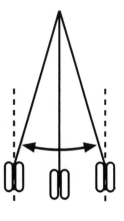

Gyroscopic stability comes from inertia. Inertia is how when something is moving it keeps going until something turns it or stops it, like gravity or a wall. Think of some guy on skates rolling down the sidewalk towards a corner. He can't stop, so at the corner he grabs a light pole and it whips him around. First off, he's got some inertia going. He's flying along and since nothing is stopping him or turning him he's continuing in a straight line. Then he grabs the pole. Again, he's not stopping so he keeps going, but since his arm is not going to stretch and is attached to his shoulder and the pole, it turns him.

Each molecule in your yo is like the guy on skates, it wants to go forward, but they're all attached to each other and to the axle. Which means they can't keep going straight because they're being turned (think of the axle as the light pole).

Next picture a big ferris wheel, except this ferris wheel is spinning really fast. Just like the molecules in your yo and the guy on skates, the boxes on the ferris wheel would be shooting straight except for the fact that they're bolted to the spokes of this thing and the spokes are attached at the hub (axle). So they want to go forward ,but they're being pulled down, then back, then up, then forward. That's the path that the boxes are on; it's not straight because the spokes are exerting a force on them and that's the way they're going. You'll notice that the path they're on is a flat plane. They're going, forward, down, back, and up, but not side to side. If we wanted a box to go sideways we'd have to apply a force to it. Again, it's going straight and the spoke is turning it down and if we wanted it to turn again, this time to the side, we'd have to apply another force.

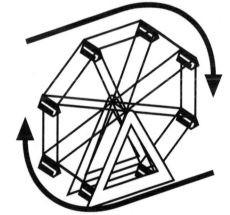

In a yo, all the molecules are attached together like how the boxes were bolted to the spokes of the ferris wheel. That force is in place and it keeps the molecules moving in a circle (around the axle).

Next let's add a new force, it could be anything gravity, the wind, charging rhino... but for this mental experiment we'll use a finger. I've got my yo in a good sleeper at the bottom of the string and then I poke it with my other finger. (this one you can actually do) What happens is that the whole yo moves to the side but it doesn't change its angle. This is because of momentum, yet another topic that takes up entire college educations, but that I will breeze over in a paragraph. Momentum is mass in motion. If something has mass (as in you can touch it and weigh it) and it's moving, it has momentum. The more it weighs and/or the faster it's going the more momentum it has. A 2 ton truck going 20 miles per hour is going to have more momentum than a 1 ton car going 20 m.p.h.. And that 1 ton car going 20 m.p.h. is going to have more momentum than a 1 ton car going 10 m.p.h..

So we've got this yo that we'll say weighs 4 ounces and is spinning at about 35 miles per hour. The fact that it's spinning tells us that half of the yo is going down while half of the yo is going up and half of the yo is going forward while the other half is going backwards. So we have 2 ounces of plastic going one way at 35 m.p.h. while 2 ounces of plastic go the other way at 35 m.p.h.. The whole thing is balanced.

2 oz going forward

2 oz going up

1 oz 1 oz 1 oz 1 oz

2 oz going down

2 oz going back

When you turn or tilt a spinning yo, you're changing the angle of the spin which means you're changing the path that the molecules are moving on. So you need as much force as it takes to change the course of 4 ounces of plastic moving at 35 m.p.h..

Now to move the yo to the side you need as much force as it

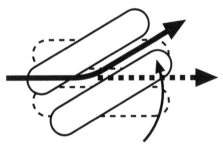

takes to scoot 4 ounces of plastic that aren't moving. Again, it's spinning and the spinning forces are balancing themselves out, so as long as the yo moves as a whole, that motion has canceled itself out.

When I apply the force of my finger against the side of the yo, the whole thing moves to the side because that is easier than tilting or turning it. Force goes into the equation and comes out via the path of least resistance. Imagine you're in a tug of war, one of you is standing on dirt and the other person is standing on a greased piece of plastic. The force goes in as you two pulling and will come out as someone moving. Who do you think is going to be pulled to who? Same thing when I poke the yo. Force goes in as me poking it and comes out as the thing moving instead of turning or tilting.

As the yo slows down it loses speed which means it loses momentum. Eventually the amount of momentum will get low enough that turning the yo will require less force than moving the whole thing. That's when your yo falls over and dies.

So you've thrown a sleeper. The yo is spinning and gyroscopic stability is holding its angle. This gives you the plane of the yo. The plane is in line with the string gap and extends out in all directions. You want to keep all of the yo's movement and the string on this plane. This way everything is lined up so string hits are easier (possible) and there's as little friction as possible.

"Keeping the plane" is keeping everything on the plane. "Breaking the plane" is when you move things off of the plane. Like if I lifted the puck off of the hockey table, I'd be breaking plane. The yo has its gyro-stability in effect so the angle of it won't change, but you'll still be unaligned. And if the plane isn't straight, gravity will keep you off of the plane.

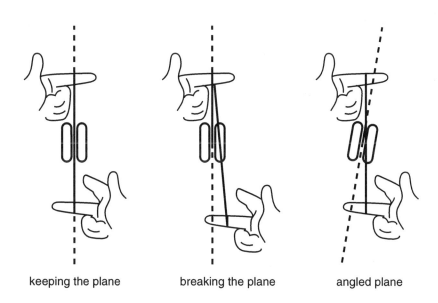

keeping the plane   breaking the plane   angled plane

11.
Talk
the Talk

This is a quick rundown of words that are used to define each other in this section and the rest of the book.

Hold- the triangular position of the string at any given time around your finger(s) and the yo. Anytime you're not doing a move you are said to be in a hold. A hold is a certain configuration of the string. When you're doing a trick you're going from hold to hold to hold simply because you keep changing the position of the string relative to itself, your fingers and the yo.

Move-anything you do with your hands or to a hold. Moves turn one hold into another hold. They're classified as neutral, one-way, zero, single, multi. Morph and tumble are examples of moves.

Mount-one of a dozen different hold/move combos that first gets the yo onto the string.

QYT- Quantum Yo Theory. The idea that yo tricks can be broken down into a series of holds and the moves that we use to get from one hold to the next.

Transcribe-to write something out. A transcription is what you get when you transcribe something.

Corner-anywhere in the path of the string where the thing bends. Usually this means your fingers and yo collectively, but if you start using other things, like throwing a trapeze over a hand rail, that's a corner too.

Side-space between 2 corners. Note: a side without string is still a side, that's why "sides" are different from "segs".

Seg- short for segment, a stretch of string between 2 corners

TFY note-the transcription of a hold using the TFY transcription method. Or the write up of a trick as an ordered list of mounts, holds and moves.

Quantum what? Well let me start by giving you a brief version of Quantum mechanics (So brief that in 200 words I'll talk about the theories that explain light, black holes, time and space).

Quantum mechanics is the study of the stuff that makes up the stuff that makes up everything. Einstein and his buddies discovered that light and energy aren't smooth continuous things, they're made up of units, bits. As in you can have a quadzillion of these little things or a quadzillion and one, but you can't have quadzillion and a half. The word "quantum" was used referring to the idea that these things came in a "quantity". And "mechanics" was used to refer to the people that clean their fuel injectors. Sorry, bad joke.

Now when you get as small as we're talking, reality changes. One of the things about these little bits is that you can only tell where they are or what they're doing. You can't tell both. Now if this sounds screwed up, it is. But that's science.

One of the other things that came from all this is that energy and matter (as in anything that is real) are the same thing. So the idea is that atoms are just this swirling around. They don't know exactly what is swirling around, all they can see its swirling. To badly paraphrase Gary Zukav, "They can't tell the dancer from the dance."

Quantum Yo Theory is the idea that all of our wacky freestyle action and tricks can be broken down into "quantum". In this book, I'll give you a run down of the 20 holds that have less than 6 segs (21 really, but that last one is useless to us, so I only mention it once) and the 13 things you can do to them. Now like quantums, you can tell what they are or what they're doing, but not both. Of course with quantums it has to do with the laws of the universe and the fact that they're smaller than light. With yos it just has to do with the fact that you'd have to stop freestyling to measure the position and when you stop freestyling you aren't freestyling.

Now these 21 holds aren't just the 21 different shapes I've seen while busting moves, they are the 21 possible builds. They can be stretched and warped and shifted and not look like themselves, but if at any point you just freeze while you're freestyling, you're string will be in one of these 21. If you aren't, then you've got more than 6 segs, a mutation (but that is still some kind of hold), or one of us is lying.

But most importantly the reason that freestyle is based on Quantum theory is that when you're really freestyling-- Now I'm talking about when you're genuinely "freestyling", fiend style, Zen style-- it's not position, move, position, move... The positions and the moves blend. The dancer and the dance are the same thing. It's all very Kung Fu.

Throwhand and Freehand

Which ever hand you have your yo tied to is your "throwhand" and which ever hand isn't tied to anything (the other one, hopefully) is your "freehand".

If you're right handed, chances are your throwhand will be your right hand (left if you're a south paw). We use "throwhand" and "freehand" for a couple reasons. One it's easier for lefties to translate. And even though it may sound confusing while you're reading this, when you get down to doing these things and talking shop with other fiends it is actually easier to understand. We also use these words so mutants with two left hands and aliens with three hands can keep up.

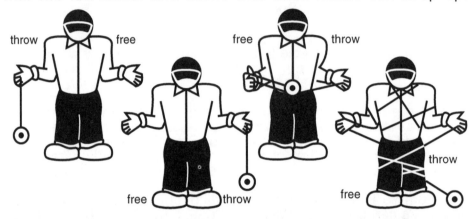

Out and In

Out and In are used to describe a hand by position. (This isn't as confusing as it seems, trust me). Whenever you're in a hold, one hand is going to be near your body and one will be away from your body. The one near your body is IN and the one away from your body is OUT.

The hand near you, inside the trick is IN. Away from you, outside the trick in OUT.

≈ 22 ≈

Backside/Frontside

Backside and Frontside refer to holds. Anytime you're in a hold and your freehand, yo and everything else is in front of your throw hand, you're in a frontside hold. In FRONT of your throwhand is Frontside. In FRONT--Frontside.

When your freehand, yo and everything else is behind your throwhand, you're in a backside hold. In BACK of your throwhand is Backside. In BACK--Backside.

FRONTSIDE

To say it in shop talk: If your freehand is out, you're in a frontside hold. If your throwhand is out, your in a backside hold.

To say it in lawyer-speak: If your throwhand is between your body and your freehand, you are in a frontside hold. If your freehand is between your body and your throwhand, then you are in a backside hold.

BACKSIDE

Why this matters:

1) Whenever you do any neutral single move (tumbles and morphs) and some of the one-way single moves, you change sides.
2) Any trick can be performed from the opposite side.
3) Every hold has a frontside and a backside version. They look different, but are actually the same hold.
4) Moves are sometimes referred to as "mix" or "match" because a forward rotation from a frontside hold gives you the same hold as a reverse rotation from a backside hold. (In case you can't figure it out: Fs.+Forward=Match, Bs.+Backwards=Match, Fs.+Backwards=Mix, and Bs.+Forward=Mix)
5) 'Cause I said so. Don't talk back!

Note: When doing sidestyle stuff, backside is when you end up with your arms crossed. But I'll talk about that in the Sidestyle section.

Whenever your yo crosses the line of your two hands you change sides. This is why whenever you do any neutral move and some of the one-way single moves you change sides. In those tricks the hand-to-hand line crosses the yo.

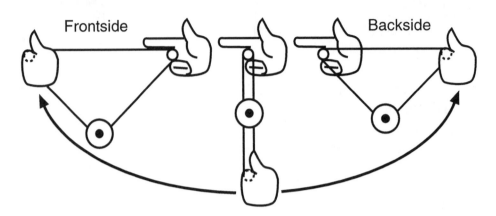

If you're lost, picture a line that goes from your throwfinger to your freefinger and just goes on in either direction. That's a hand-to-hand line, like the line between the two goal posts that the ball has to cross in any goalie sport. Now reread the last paragraph.

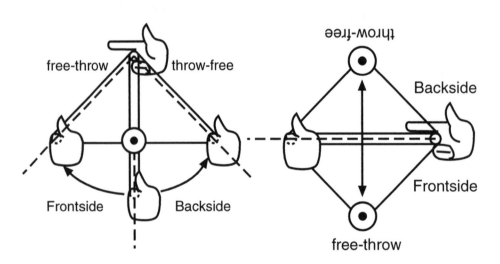

Another time this happens is when you hop, dunk, or lap (a few multi moves) your yo. With those tricks your yo is actually above your hands at some point and when it goes from a hold below your hands to a hold above your hands, it's crosses that line and moves into a different hold that is inverted and has the opposite side. Now, unless you've figured out a way to defy gravity or are freestyling in a plane that is plummeting towards the earth, an inverted hold will last only as long as it takes for your yo to fall back down. That's why moves like a hop or a dunk are actually multi moves instead of single moves.

Rotation

Rotation is the direction of a tumble, morph, roll, twist, sling, etc. A move where you rotate your fingers out away from you is a forward rotation. A move where you rotate your fingers in towards you is a backward rotation. If you think of the trick as a wheel, the direction of the wheel turning would be the same thing.

In lawyer-speak: When your higher finger moves from the in position to the out position, it is a forward rotation. When your higher finger moves from the out position to the in position, it is a backwards rotation.

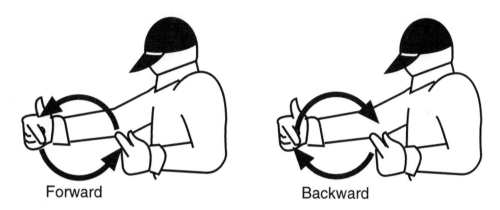

Forward   Backward

Now in a move the only thing that matters to the trick is where your fingers go in relation to each other and the yo. So as long as my in finger moves over my out finger into the out position, it's a forward rotation.

A quick and easy way to add a little finesse and style and to smooth out your moves is to move your fingers in relation to each other. In other words, for a forward rotation you can keep your in finger where it is and move your out finger under it or you can keep your out finger where it is and move your in finger over it or you can move them both together. It's all the same rotation.

forward   forward   forward

──────── *notice that they're all forward* ────────

≈ 25 ≈

TFY transcription is how we write out holds (and tricks). "Note" is short for notation, as in what we get when we transcribe a hold. It's not hard. There are 3 points in any hold, your throwhand, freehand and the yo. Throw, **F**ree, **Y**o.

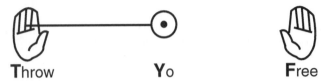

Throw   **Y**o   **F**ree

A note starts out with "Fs." or "Bs.", they stand for frontside and backside. If the hold is in sidestyle you put a "S" in front of it. So "SFs." is a sidestyle frontside hold, "SBs." is sidestyle backside, "Fs." is regular frontside and "Bs." is regular backside.

After that are a series of letters, sometimes with a number in parenthesis at the end. The number is just for reference. All holds with 5 or less segs are numbered and in the "Holds" section of this book. It starts with a sleeper which is #0, since it really doesn't have a TFY note (the string doesn't bend), and ends with #20.

The letters are where the string bends around a corner. To get these letters you trace or follow the where the string goes between it's 2 ends, starting at your throwhand and ending at your yo. After it leaves your throwhand it's first bend will be either your freehand (F) or the yo (Y). That's your first letter. Then the next corner it hits will be the next letter. If it first goes to your freehand, the next letter would be either "Y" (if it then went around the yo) or "T" (if it went back around your throwfinger). If it had gone around the yo first it could then go to your freehand, F, or back to your throwhand, T. Then to the next corner and so on. This continues until the path of the string ends at the axle.

The note is point to point to point, etc. It's the position of the path. It doesn't matter what the string does at a corner, it only depends which corner it is, "T", "F", or "Y". So if I have it wrapped, pinched, wound around three times, off a different finger of that hand... it doesn't matter to the note. This means that you won't have the same letter next to itself in a note. It also means that notes won't start with "T" or end with "Y". Since those are the ends of the string, even if you have a wrap around them, the string has still ended at that point.

For example (I know you've been waiting for those two words): Let's say I'm in a hold and I trace the string first to the yo, then it wraps around my free finger and then ends back at the yo. That's a YF hold. The string started at the knot and went first to the yo so the first letter is Y. Then it went up to your free hand so the next letter is F. Then it ended. You're left with Y and F, equaling YF.

To do it again: let's say we follow our string this time out to our freefinger (F), down to the yo (Y), back up to our throwhand (T) and then ends. It'd be a FYT.

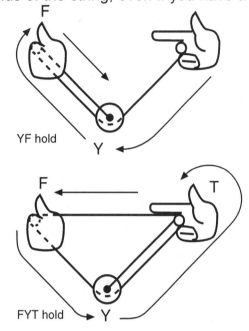

TFY transcription is also used on tricks. When you transcribe a trick what you're doing is listing, in order, the mount, moves and holds that you go through. First is either the mount or "sleeper" that you start with "-" (dash) the hold you end up with. Tricks are listed mount-hold, move-hold, move-hold, move-hold... exit move. It's somewhere between sheet music and empirical formula. But there's a "Tricks" section, so I'll leave it for then.

A seg, short for segment, is a length of string between 2 corners. If you're in a straight sleeper, the whole string is one seg. If you fold the string over your freehand, you end up with 2 segs. Fold it over 2 more times and you'll have 4 segs. You get the idea.

Segs can be referred to by the 2 corners they're between. A seg that goes from your throwhand to your yo would be a TY seg. You want to list the points in the order that the string gets to them. So if the string goes from your yo, around your freehand then back to the yo, the first one would be YF and the second one would be FY. If it sounds complicated don't worry, it's not and it doesn't come up that often.

There are 2 specific seg names, "Base" and "End". The base seg is the first seg; the one that starts with the knot around your finger. The end seg is the last seg; the one that ends around the axle of the yo.

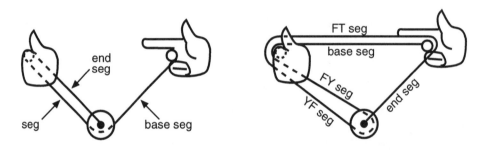

Holds are also referred to by how many segs they have. A 3 seg hold has three segs in it. For example, a F hold has 2 segs while a FTYF has 5 segs. The note for a hold will have one more seg than it does letters. So a 3 seg hold will have 2 letters in its note.

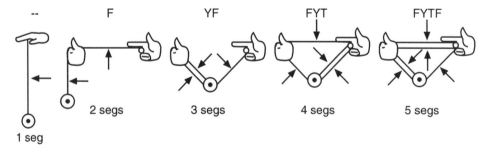

In this book I only bothered giving write up to holds with less than 6 segs. Every time you add a seg to a hold, they all get shorter. And the more segs you have, usually the more times you go around the axle and the more times you go around the axle the more friction you have, the faster it slows down. After 5 segs it becomes more of a pain than it's worth.

Mutations

Mutations are holds where the string doesn't wrap in nice easy segs. The most common mutations are a string wrapping around a finger or the yo an extra or full time before it moves on to the next corner in the hold. Another version of this is if the string comes into a corner on the wrong side and goes out on the opposite side.

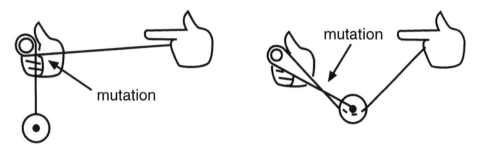

The reason that mutations are bad is that they choke up your freestyle action by making it impossible to slide the string over your finger and messing up transforming holds in the case of extra wraps or bad wraps. And when it happens around your yo, you get knots around the axle. Basically they're a pain in the @$$.

There are some tricks that work by jumping into and quickly out of a mutation. They are few and far between, but can be cool.

Hits (and Pulls)

Real simply, whenever your yo lands on, transfers to, jumps to, bisects, etc.. some string, it's a hit. Mounts and tumbles are hits.

The term hit is also used to measure freestyle tricks; as in how many hits are there in the trick. Thus a "3 hit trick" is one where the yo is threaded, dropped, transferred or whatever onto the string three times during the course of the trick. Segs have nothing to do with it, for example, a tumble onto two segs is still only one hit.

The term hit usually refers to the yo, but it can be used to refer to a finger. If that's the case it's, "...hit that seg with your finger."

"Pull" is also used to refer to when your finger hits, bends, bisect, transfers, etc. the string. Typically it will be used in regards to "pulling a seg".

Jargon- a specialized, informal vocabulary

Closed Hold-a hold that has segs between all three corners so the string makes a full triangle. FYT and TFYT are examples of closed holds.

Open Hold- a hold where there is a side without any segs. TFT and YFYT are open holds.

Knucklebiter-when the yo snags or catches and comes back in the middle of a complicated hold or trick and smacks you in the knuckles. Hurts like hell and usually incites many obscenities.

Old "Skool"-the school of thought on yoing that is based on tricks that are more predominantly single move, novel, and loop-based. Old Skoolers usually prefer fixed axles.

New School-the school of thought on yoing that is based on Quantum Yo Theory, freestyle action, and who's tricks are predominantly sleeper based. New Schoolers usually prefer transaxles.

Conquistayoers-yoers that are into contests, competing and expanding their list of tricks.

Fiend-yoers that don't believe in organized contests, hold to the Zen of yoing and are into undefined action and tricks.

Old Master- a term that fiends use to respectfully refer to those who came before them. (This is unrelated to the title "National Master", although the National Masters are considered Old Masters)

Landing-successfully completing a trick. If you finish the trick with the yo in your hand you've landed it.

Dead- when your yo is at the end of the string and not spinning. If it runs out of spin, it is said to "die". If you stop it spinning you've "killed" it. And thus the birth of dead tricks, like "Walk the dead dog", "Rock the dead baby", and "Around the dead world". To take the joke even further, do a "Dead trapeze" (side single mount) and when the yo hits the string and promptly falls off because it's not spinning, you can say, "What did you expect? A dead circus guy can't hold onto a trapeze."

III.
Mounts

To do any freestyle trick worth doing, you have to get the yo on the string. A mount is your first hit and how you get going.

There are 3 basic ways you can get on the string (for sub-6 seg action): single, double, and split. They give us our 3 starting holds, F(1), YFYT(17), and FYT(6). You can get on at the top or the bottom of each of these and each has 2 sides. Thus we have 12 different basic mounts. That simple. (it actually is, read on)

Top mounts are where the hand that is last to touch the yo is above the other. With top mounts you have some time to line it up, this is because the yo is hanging and sleeping and where it's headed can be moved around. With bottom mounts, you don't have that luxury since the yo is moving; you have to just hit it.

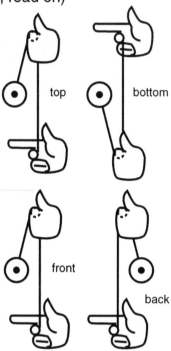

Mounts, like anything else, have two sides: front and back. Front mounts are when the yo gets on the front of the string. Back mounts are when the yo gets on the string from behind it. Each factor in a mount has an effect on whether you end up with a frontside or backside hold and it'd be too much to write out in one place, so be aware and just read it in the write ups.

Getting the yo on the string is only part of the mount. But it's the biggest part of the mount so I want to take a second to discuss. Now we've already talked about planes and they are no more important than in that first mount.

String to string gap-- the essence of a mount. The string gap creates a plane, for the string to get into the gap it has to line up with that plane. The gyroscopic stability of a spinning yo is going to hold the plane in place. The end seg of the string is always going to be straight up and down (gravity will take care of that). And since the rest of the segs have a common point with the end seg (which ever finger it's coming off of), you have to have a good straight up and down sleeper to get it on the string.

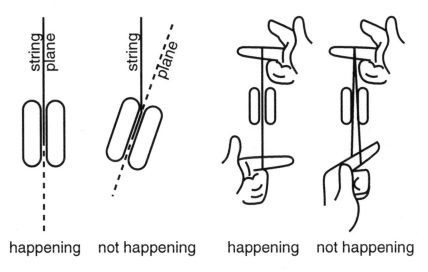

happening   not happening   happening   not happening

When you're doing a double mount (or anytime you're hitting multiple segs) you have to make sure that the extra segs are all on the same plane. This is easy enough, just make sure that you keep your fingers perpendicular to the string plane and the strings wrapped evenly around.

With bottom mounts the yo is swinging up and onto the string. There's no time to line it up. But fear not, if you have a straight throw, keep your fingers perpendicular to the string, and pull the string smoothly, the yo should stay on the plane. This is very important: you have to make sure that you let some slack into the string. On bottom mounts, as soon as the yo is up and on the string, give it slack so it can carry through. Otherwise it'll bounce right off.

Top single is the first and easiest mount. Start with a good sleeper. Fold the string over your freefinger, line up the string and the string gap and push the string into it. Not complicated.

For a front top single, start with your free finger behind the string so you can fold the string back and have the base seg behind the yo. Fold it over, line up the string gap and carry your throwfinger forward and into a Bs.YF(3) hold.

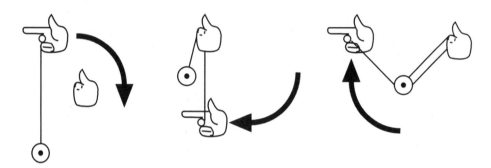

For a back top single, start with you free finger in front of the string, wrap your throw finger over it, line up the string gap and pull your throw finger back into a Fs.YF(3).

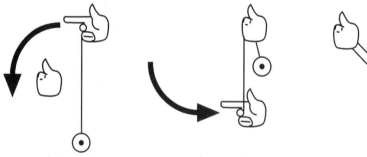

When folding the string over, you want your free finger to pull the string a third of its length from the yo. The closer to the yo your free hand is when you first pull it, the higher it'll be when you're feeding it onto the base seg. If you're free finger is in the top half of the string when you first fold it over, it will be above the yo when you try and put it on the string (no string there, no mount.)

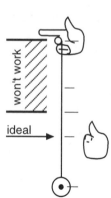

Bottom Single

A bottom single is when you pull the string of a sleeper and catch the yo on the gap as it swings up from the pull. As far as raw movement, you're basically doing an overscoop from nothing (see multi moves).

For a front bottom single, start with your free finger in front of a sleeper. Bring your finger down and hit the string a third of the way up from the yo. If you do this right, the tug on the string should cause the yo to swing up and if you keep everything in line, it should swing right up string to string gap. When it hits, sink your hands in a little to give the string some slack so the yo can carry through. As the yo is going back, bring your freefinger forward into a Fs. YF(3). If you do this right, the whole thing is really fluid.

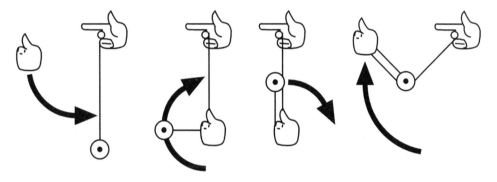

For a back bottom single, start with your finger behind the sleeper. Push your free finger forward into the back of the string, the yo swings up, give it slack, carry it through and scoop your free finger back.

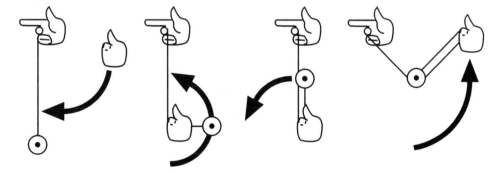

As with a front top single, you want to put your free finger a third or less of the way up the string and no more than a half.

A top double is where you fold the string over your free finger and then again over your throw finger and put the yo on the two segs that are between your fingers. The yo is hanging off the top finger, but this time the top finger is your throw finger.

For a front top double, start with your free finger behind the sleeper and bring it into the string so you fold the string back over it. Then fold the remaining string (end seg) back over your throw finger. Bring your free finger down and line up the string gap and the two segs behind it. Put it on them and scoop your free finger forward into a Fs.YFYT(17).

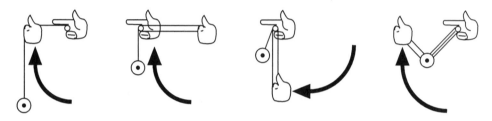

For a back top double, start with your free finger in front of the sleeper. Fold it forward over your free finger, then forward again over your throw finger. Bring your free finger down and put the yo on the double segs. Then scoop through into a Bs.YFYT(17).

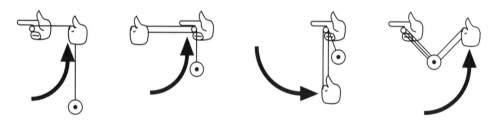

For a top double you want your first fold to be 3/5 of the way up the string (just above halfway). Your second fold would be at a third of the remaining string.

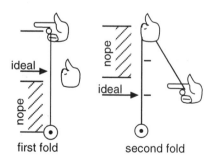

first fold   second fold

For a bottom double you fold the string over your free finger then bring your throw finger down and pull the string so it swings the yo up and over. Catch the yo on both strings, give it some slack and scoop it up with your throw finger.

A front bottom double starts with your free finger in front of the sleeper. Fold the thing forward over it; your free finger should hit 3/5 of the way from the yo (just above half). As your throwfinger comes over in the fold, bring it down and hit the remaining string a third of the way up from the yo. Just like a bottom single, the yo should swing up and into the string. Catch it on both segs, making sure to give it some slack, and carry your throw finger forward and up into a Bs.YFYT(17).

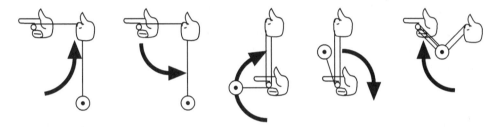

Back bottom doubles start with folding the string back over your free finger which is behind the sleeper. Bring your throw finger down and into the string, swinging the yo up and into the string. Give it some slack as you bring your throwfinger back into a Fs.YFYT(17).

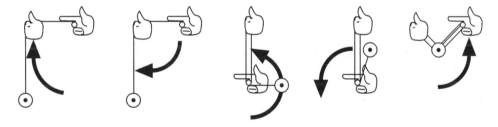

The finger placement for the folds in a bottom double are the same as for a top double (except the last one is more of a string pivot than a regular fold). So give a look to the last page for the picture of 3/5 and 1/3 string pulls.

A top split is the same as a top double, you do the free finger fold then the throwfinger folds (also at the 3/5 and 1/3 marks), but instead of the string being right on top of the fingerloop, you shift it out towards the tip of your finger so it's off plane. When you line up the string gap, line it up just on the seg that goes from this corner down (TF not the base seg). Feed the string gap onto that seg and carry your free finger through.

For a front top split, start with your free finger behind the sleeper, fold it back over it, then carry your free finger over and fold the string over your throw finger, making sure that the second fold is at least a knuckle out from the finger loop. Line up the FT seg (not the base seg) vertically with the string gap, feed it on and carry your free finger forward into a Fs.FYT(6).

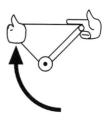

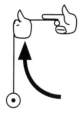 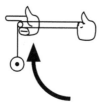 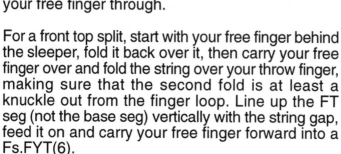

A back top split starts with folding a sleeper forward over your free finger that is in front of it. Then you fold it forward again over your throw finger, making sure to separate the string wraps. Carry your free finger through, feeding the TF seg (not the base seg) into the string gap and into a Bs.FYT(6).

  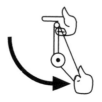 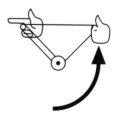

A bottom split, like a top split, is very similar to its double counterpart. Bottom splits fold over the free finger and then into a yo swing over the throwfinger. The difference (like with a top split) is that the corner wrap of second fold is shifted out so that the yo can be lined up to hit only one of the two segs. You then carry it through with your throw finger. Again your fingers hit at the 3/5 and 1/3 marks.

For a front bottom split, fold the sleeper forward over your free finger, then bring your throwfinger down into the end seg. Pull it with the end of your finger, so you can keep the base seg out of the way, so the yo swings up and into the string. Like with any bottom mount, give it some slack and bring your throwfinger back forward into a Bs.FYT(6).

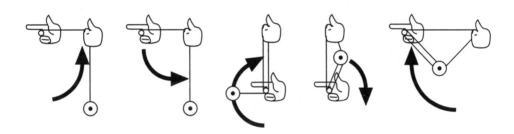

For a back bottom split, fold your string back over your free finger, then bring your throwfinger down into the string. Hit the string with the end of your finger so the yo swings up and into that seg of the string (not the base seg). Give it slack and carry your throw finger back into a Fs.FYT(6).

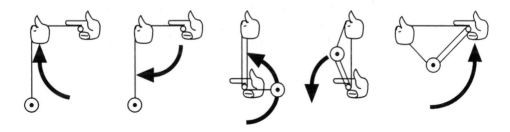

For the sake of record and interest, here are the mounts transcribed into TFY notes. If you're reading this straight through for the first time, you haven't gotten to the part that explains this stuff. But it's coming, don't worry.

Top Single-
Front: Bs.Sleeper(0), Back.Morph- Fs.F(1), Back.Tumble- Bs.YF(3)
Back: Fs.Sleeper(0), For.Morph- Bs.F(1), For.Tumble- Fs.YF(3)

Bottom Single-
Front: Fs.Sleeper(0), Free OverScoop (For.Morph/Back.Tumble)-
 Fs.YF(3)
Back: Bs.Sleeper(0), Free Overscoop (Back.Morph/For.Tumble)-
 Bs.YF(3)

Top Double-
Front: Bs.Sleeper(0), Back.Morph- Fs.F(1), Back.Morph- Bs.FT(2),
 For.Tumble- Fs.YFYT(17)
Back: Fs.Sleeper(0), For.Morph- Bs.F(1), For.Morph-FT(2),
 Back.Tumble-Bs.YFYT(17)

Bottom Double-
Front: Fs.Sleeper(0), For.Morph- Bs.F(1), Throw Overscoop (For.Morph/
 Back.Tumble)- Bs.YFYT(17)
Back: Bs.Sleeper(0), Back.Morph- Fs.F(1), Throw Overscoop
 (Back.Morph/ For.Tumble)- Fs.YFYT(17)

Top Split-
Front: Bs.Sleeper(0), Back.Morph- Fs.F(1), Back.Morph- Bs.FT(2),
 Back.Split Tumble- Fs.FYT(6)
Back: Fs.Sleeper(0), For.Morph- Bs.F(1), For.Morph- Fs.FT(2), For.Split
 Tumble- Bs.FYT(6)

Bottom Split-
Front: Fs.Sleeper(0), For.Morph- Bs.F(1), Split Throw Overscoop
 (For.Morph/ Back.Split Tumble)- Bs.FYT(6)
Back: Bs.Sleeper(0), Back.Morph- Fs.F(1), Split Throw Overscoop
 (Back.Morph/ For.Split Tumble)- Fs.FYT(6)

IV.
Moves

Moves are what you do to holds. Quantum Yo theory: It's where something is or what it's doing. Moves are what something's doing.

There are three classes of moves: zero, single, and multi. Zero moves are moves where you don't end up with a new hold. Either the hold never goes away (as in a roll or sling) or the move creates a warped version of the hold where the only way out is the way you came in (cradles and twists). Which ever, there's no change to a new hold.

Single moves are the foundation of freestyling action. They are how we transform holds into new holds. There are a couple basic ways to do it. Since holds are patterns of string around fingers and a yo, you can change 'em by adding and subtracting fingers, which are drop and pluck moves.

Now holds are triangles, but they aren't simple geometry triangles (which are just sets of three points), they are paths of a string around three points. They have direction. You can stretch, bend and warp a triangle and it'll always be that triangle, but a hold is more than a triangle. Which means that you can turn it inside out! We do this by pushing one of the corners through its opposite side; 3 corners, 3 ways to do it: Tumble, Free Morph and Throw Morph. These are our basic three single moves.

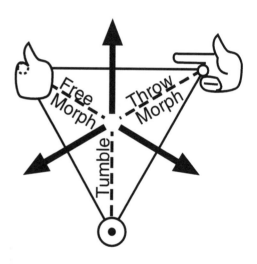

When ever you turn a hold inside out, you change its side, frontside to backside, backside to frontside. So with the exception of some drops and plucks, anytime you do a single move, the hold that you get will be the opposite side of the one you started with. For example: If you start with a frontside FYT and do a tumble, you'll end up with a backside YFT. Those moves which don't change side are called "same side" moves and are noted with a "ss".

Rotation comes into this too. Each hold has 2 versions (each side) and your move relative to that is what matters. Doing a forward move from a frontside is going to give you the same hold (opposite side) as doing the same backwards move from the backside version.

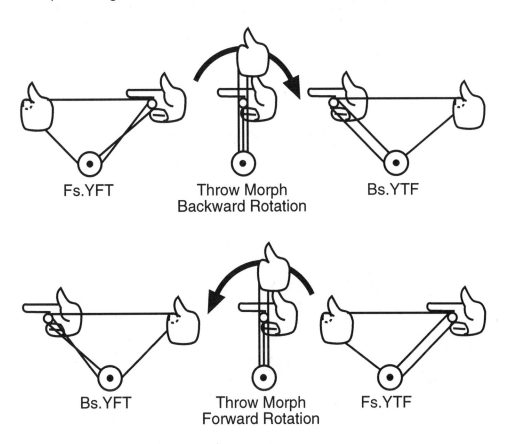

Fs.YFT   Throw Morph   Bs.YTF
                       Backward Rotation

Bs.YFT   Throw Morph   Fs.YTF
                       Forward Rotation

Here's the kicker: Tumbles are neutral, so rotation direction doesn't matter to them. But whenever you're doing a morph, if your rotation matches the side of the hold (e.g. frontside hold, forward rotation) then your free finger will be moving below your throwfinger (through the middle of the hold). And if your rotation and hold are opposites (Backside hold, forward rotation), then you'll be moving you're throw finger. This is why we transcribe morphs as "free and throw", but teach them as "forward and backward"; they're interchangeable. See, when you're on paper figuring out where you can go or recording a trick, what matters is the moves you use to get to the holds. But when you're in the heat of it and doing it, what matters is the rotation and how you're moving your fingers. It sounds confusing, but if you remember your rotations and your fingers, then you'll be fine.

So there are 3 essential ways to transform a triangle, which gives us our 3 essential moves (tumble and morphs). Again, holds are more than triangles which means that the real world creeps into our perfect little world of math and gives us different variations on these moves based on how we hit and pull the segs; namely regular (full), split and miss. Three moves and 3 variations of each, give us 9 transform moves. Then you add two fingers to add and subtract and you end up with our 13 single moves.

Multi moves are smooth bits of action that are actually 2 or more single moves, but since you can do them and shoot right through the in-between hold, they can be thought of as one move. You're actually doing 2 moves and you have an in-between hold that is the opposite side. This means that the hold you end up with after a multi move is very often the same side as the one you started with.

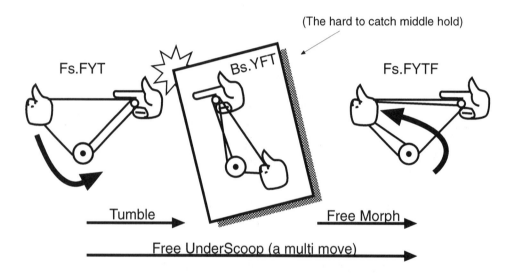

(The hard to catch middle hold)

Fs.FYT   Bs.YFT   Fs.FYTF

Tumble   Free Morph

Free UnderScoop (a multi move)

The combo of tumbles and morphs in a multi move come from the sides/ segs that you're hitting and pulling. And since the move is just the movement of your finger, the component single moves can be full, split or miss moves. For example, in the move illustrated above if you were slick enough to substitute a split free morph in for the free morph, you could end up with a YTF(9) instead of the FYTF(11).

Zero moves and multi moves aren't given write up in the holds section or on the subway map. This is because zero moves can be just thrown in at almost any point and multis are actually singles. So if you're using the map or working out tricks by the hold write ups, look for the single moves that combine into a multi and just fit zeros in where ever.

Tumble

A tumble is a move where you move your bottom hand under the yo. You can tumble a hold in either direction, forward or backward, but either way you'll end up in the same new hold.

For a forward tumble, bring your Out finger under the yo to the In position, while you move your In finger over them all to the Out position.

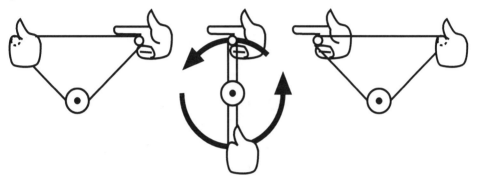

For a backward tumble, bring your In finger under the yo to the Out position and your Out hand over everything else into the In position.

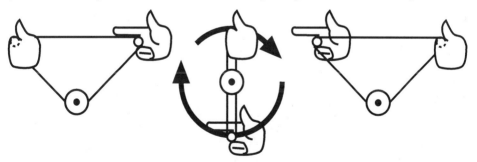

For a regular, full tumble you want to catch all the segs of a side in the transfer (when your yo passes to the other side).

The reason that both forward and backward tumbles create the same holds is that tumbling a hold is effectively inverting it. If you moved your yo straight up between your hands you'd end up with the same hold as you do when you tumble. So it really doesn't matter which way you go, you're going to a place between them anyway. When one finger goes under the yo, the yo hits the FT side of the hold.

There are two morphs, Free and Throw, each one will give you a different next hold. They're named for which ever finger is going through the middle of the hold.

So unlike with tumbles, which way you go will matter. Like I said at the beginning of this part, if you're in a frontside hold, a free morph will be a forward rotation and a throw morph a backward rotation. If you're in a backside hold, a free morph will be backward and a throw morph forward. (Free morphs match side and rotation, Throw morphs mix side and rotation)

For a forward morph, move your Out finger under your In finger, but above the yo, and into the In position as you move your In finger over everything else into the Out position.

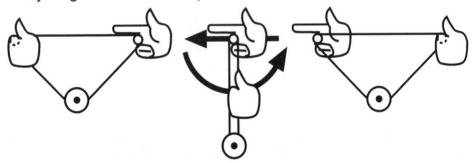

For a backward morph, move your In finger under your Out finger, but above the yo, and into the Out position as you move your Out finger, over everything else into the In position

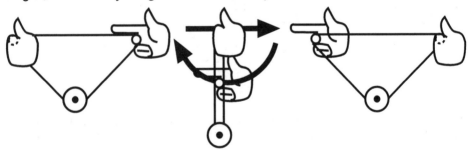

For a full morph, make sure you pull all of the layers of a side (which is of course easier than pulling only some of the layers, but we'll get to that soon enough).

In a morph, the yo doesn't actually leave the string at any time. This is why morphs aren't considered hits when you're counting them for a trick. (sorry)

For a split tumble, there has to be at least two segs between your fingers, otherwise you're doing a regular tumble. A split tumble is where you're doing a tumble, but instead of catching all of the segs in the yo, you only catch some of them (one for our purposes)

When you're doing this, make sure that you hit only outside segs. If you hit an inside layer, you're going to get a mutation. Base seg are almost always on the inside so they almost always cause a mutation. Be careful. And if you figure out a way to tumble onto the end seg, call me.

To do a split tumble you have to break plane. You break plane in one of two ways depending on what you're trying to split.

When you're splitting segs that involve a string that goes all the way around a hold (note combos with F, Y, and T), most closed holds, you split your layers by separating the wraps on your finger and rocking your finger.

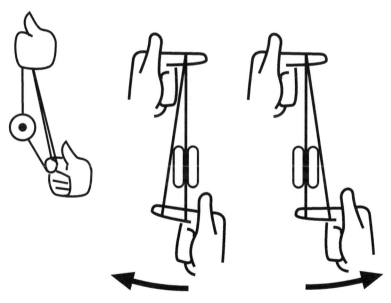

This is why I recommend putting your knot on your base knuckle rather than your middle knuckle; it gives you more to work with when you start doing split moves.

When you're trying to split segs that come from the string coming off of one finger, around the other and then back to the first (FTF or TFT note combos), then what you have to do is pivot your bottom finger so the width of your finger becomes the separation. If you slide in an extra finger, like if you do it right after a cradle, then you can add some extra width and that makes it a little easier.

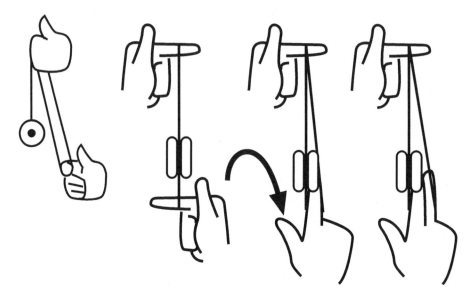

Miss Tumble

A miss tumble is the same as a split tumble, but instead of only hitting some of the segs, you hit none of them. You break plane with all of the segs. So what you're effectively doing is getting the yo off of the string it's sitting on.

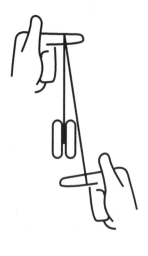

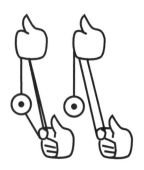

A split morph, as you may guess by the name, is just like a regular morph except that, like a split tumble, you aren't pulling all of the segs. Hence the term "split".

Like all split moves, if you pull an inside seg on split morph you're going to get a mutation and if you pull a base seg, you probably will. You also have to break plane to do this move, but since there's no hit involved, it's pretty easy.

A forward split morph is using your Out finger, under your In finger to finally end up in the In position. But instead of neatly pulling all of the segs in a side, you only pull one or some of them.

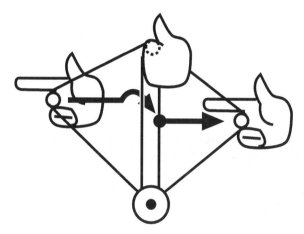

A backward split morph is moving your In finger, under your Out finger but over the yo, pulling the outside seg, and ending up in the Out position. Again, a morph where you dodge the inside segs.

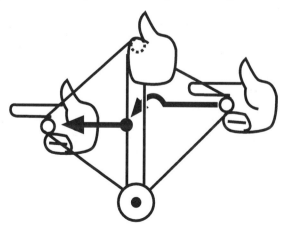

Miss Morph

A miss morph is where you move your hands through the morph move, break plane and not pull any segs. Whenever you do this, the hand that will be moving under the other one is going to be your throwhand, otherwise you're just doing a drop (next move). Mutations also love this move (the big reason why it's real rare), so fair warning.

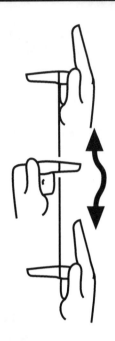

Free Finger Drop

Real easy, you drop all of the segs off of your freehand finger. Just yank your freefinger out of the hold and let 'em fall. This move will give you either a straight sleeper, a mutation or a YT(4) hold. If you go into 6 and more seg holds you can drop back down to YTYT(20), the phantom 21st 5 seg hold.

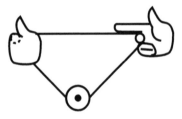
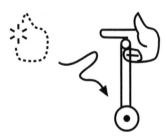

Throw Finger Drop

Just let all the string on your throw finger fall. Obviously you won't lose your base seg (if you do, you have other problems). Like a split morph, this move is a breeding ground for mutations, so watch out. This move is also a same-side move, so if you drop a frontside hold you'll get another frontside hold.

Pluck

The opposite of a throw finger drop is a pluck. A pluck is when you reach in with your throw finger, hook another seg onto your finger and return to the position that your fingers were in. This move is bordering on being a double move (it's something like a 1.5 move). But since the yo really doesn't cross the hand-hand line, it's a single. It's also a same-side move (another reason I want to call it a multi move).

Unless it says otherwise, a pluck is done with your throwfinger, but Free finger plucks do exist. They exist in 2 forms. The first is adding a freefinger to a YT(4) hold (see that hold's write up for details). The other way is if you want to add a seg to your freehand if it already has some string on it. The action for this one would be just like a regular throwfinger pluck, but to do it effectively you'd drop what segs you have and then be doing a YT(4) pluck. So then you're doing a multi move, which I'd just as soon leave as 2 smaller moves; they aren't smooth enough together to treat otherwise.

OverScoop

An overscoop is where you take a finger, run it over (go fig) the yo, and then scoop around it and bring your finger back to where it started. You can't hesitate on this move. If you do, it gets clunky and becomes much harder. If you slide your finger through it quickly you can get a little recoil jump in your yo off the string which makes it easier and smoother.

Free Overscoop=Free Morph+Tumble
Throw Overscoop=Throw Morph+Tumble

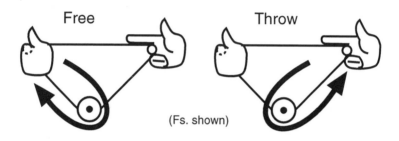

Free   Throw

(Fs. shown)

UnderScoop

Related to the overscoop but different. As the name would suggest, this time you run your finger under the yo and then bring it back to its original position. Like I said earlier, you can't hesitate on scoops. If you slide right into the scoop you can get a little hop and a split second of hangtime in the yo which'll let you slip right under it. Real smooth.

Free Under scoop=Tumble+Free Morph
Throw Underscoop=Tumble+Throw Morph

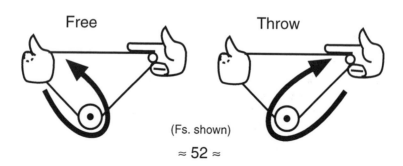

Free   Throw

(Fs. shown)

Hop

A hop is when you give the string a little outward jerk with your fingers so the yo pops up through the top FT side and then continues around to underneath. Forward hops are when the yo goes over your out finger, backwards are over your in hand. But again, they're noted according to which finger they jump over. You can pick where it goes by tuning how hard you pull your fingers compared to each other and by rocking the hold a little forward or backward. Not hard, just practice. If you're hopping into FT segs, you have to give the hold some slack real quick, otherwise it won't carry through. If it's an open top hold, then who cares.

Free Hop=Tumble+Free Morph
Throw Hop=Tumble+Throw Morph

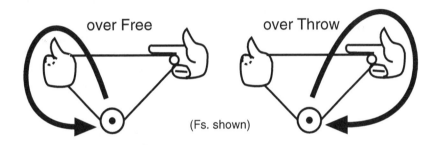

over Free   over Throw

(Fs. shown)

Dunk

A dunk is the opposite of a hop. Instead of going through the top and then coming around the side, you swing the yo around the side, up, and then drop in the top. Again, you have to swing your yo out for a forward and swing it in for a backward. Be generous with the slack in the hold.

Free Dunk=Free Morph+Tumble
Throw Dunk=Throw Morph+Tumble

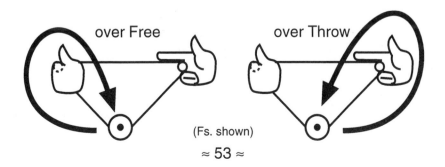

over Free   over Throw

(Fs. shown)

A lap is a move where you run a corner all the way around the hold and back to where it started. Laps are referred to as "mix" and "match". If you haven't caught on yet, that means that if you're in a frontside hold you'll be doing a forward rotation for a "match" and a backward rotation for a "mix". Backside gives you forward for "mix" and backward for "match". The drawings below are all Frontside.

Throw Lap

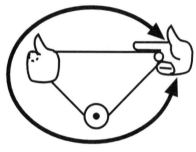

Mix Throw Lap=Tumble+Free Morph
Match Throw Lap=Free Morph+Tumble

Free Lap

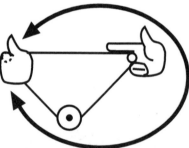

Mix Free Lap=Throw Morph+Tumble
Match Free Lap=Tumble+Throw Morph

Yo Lap

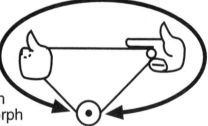

Mix Yo Lap=Free Morph+Throw Morph
Match Yo Lap=Throw Morph+Free Morph

On the yo lap, the move to get the yo going is the same as a dunk, but instead of dropping it in the middle, you carry it all the way around. I'm sure you could've figured that one out, I was just illustrating the motion it takes to get it rolling.

On the free and throw laps, make sure you leave enough slack so that the yo doesn't follow your finger around. If you do that you're doing a roll and not a lap.

Unraveling is an exit move, that is it ends in straight sleeper. Real easy, when you have a hold that has the string wrapped around in a nice even way, you start it with a little move and then just pull it so the yo runs around the hold and unwraps it.

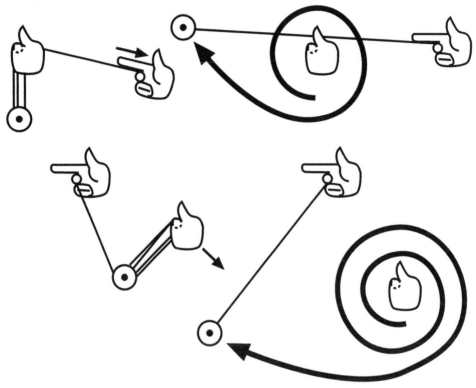

The little move to start will usually just be swinging the yo in the direction you're unraveling, but sometimes a hop will be needed to get it going.

Depending on how fast you pull the string out will determine how tight the circle is; it's something you get a feel for. I mention this because one of the big dangers of unraveling (especially when you aren't throwing the action sideways) is hitting yourself as it flings off the hold. By pulling faster at some points in the move, you can get it so the circle is actually smaller on one side. But my advice is just keep it small; often it looks cooler just spinning around your hand.

A switch stance is an unusual move because it involves the use of more than two fingers. To do it you have to shift between your middle finger and your index finger (2 on one hand + 1 on the other=3) . Basically you hop the yo off the string and as it rounds off your finger you put the one next to it in for the string to bend around and make the new corner. You end up with the same hold, but a different side

And since nothing is easy, this can be done forward or backward, top or bottom, but only for certain holds. But all of this matches up rather well with mounts, you have top and bottom, forward and backward YF(3) and YFYT(17).

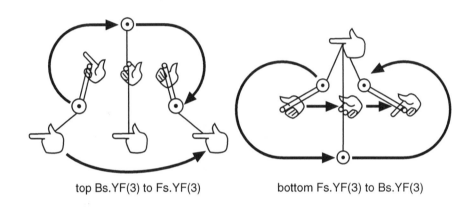

top Bs.YF(3) to Fs.YF(3)   bottom Fs.YF(3) to Bs.YF(3)

One thing that does make it a little simpler is that when your in any hold you can only go one direction. In a Bs.YF(3), whether I go top or bottom, it'll be a backwards rotation. The difference is which hand comes up and whether the yo goes over or under the hold.

Just like any multi move, you can throw in split moves for part of the move. For a switch stance, splitting a YFYT(17) is how you get FYT(6) to account for that mount. Basically you hop it and then catch only the opposite side seg.

Which ever finger is in a hold (or both) doesn't matter to the hold. A YF(3) whether it goes around the middle finger on your throw hand or the index finger on your throwhand is still a YF(3).

Grind

A grind in yo terms is when you drop the sleeping yo onto a surface and let it spin. The ever popular trick of "Walk the Dog" is simply a sleeper grinding the ground. But there is more to grinds than just stupid pet tricks.

Any hold can be lowered onto a table top, a hand rail or the person in front of you not paying attention. The best grinds are loud, hard surfaces like metal stand bases or fiber glass chairs and balance runs like straddling your string gap on a pencil or the back of a wooden chair.

For a grind you simply lower a spinning yo onto whatever you're grinding. Tip: the bigger the angle away from perpendicular to your surface the better. So straight up and down for the ground is bad, but if you come straight down on a slanted surface, it's no biggie. If you come straight down (perpendicular) on a grind 2 things work against you: first, the natural tiny jumps and bounces from the yo go straight up the string, so they're more likely to cause your yo to catch and come back. If your string is at an angle, the jumps and bounces are less into the string and more against it. Second (most important), laying out a drop lets you keep tension on the string. If you're coming straight down, anything after the yo hits the ground is slack in the string which'll make it come back. If you're lowering something in a full triangle hold, the string is already at an angle.

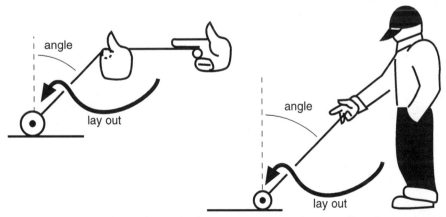

A few cool variations for grinds are reverse throws (lay it out behind you), "landing" a "Flying Saucer" (figure it out) and throwing a slanted sleeper and laying that out (it'll run to the side).

A twist is where all three corners are lined up, one finger becomes a center turning point and the other is used to spin the hold around it. This can be done either forward or backward.

For a forward twist bring your in finger up over your out finger (the yo'll line up on its own) and then pull against the string and spin the whole thing forward around your Out finger. For a backward twist, bring your out finger up over your in finger (the in will be the center) and spin. Note: there needs to be at least one seg between the finger that's going to be the top finger and the yo to pull against, otherwise you'll just be doing a really goofy morph.

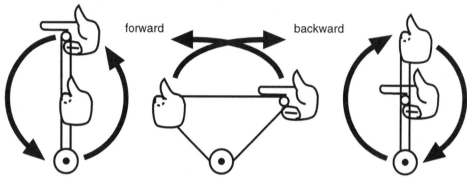

Another way to do a twist is to let the top finger be the center and the middle finger do the work. Same line up and rotations, just changing were your pivot point and power are. This way is easier to get spinning, but also easier to get messy.

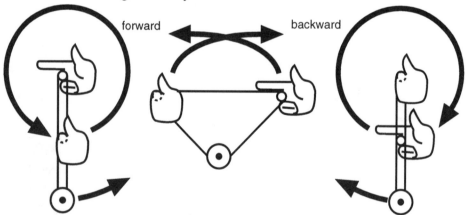

If you let your finger get ahead of the yo, you'll get the whole thing screwed up. No matter which way you do it, make sure to keep your fingers and the yo in line. If they're going around at different speeds, it gets messy and it also looks sloppy.

Roll

Rolls are similar to twists, except instead of collapsing the hold and spinning the yo like an extra limb, you simply spin the entire hold as it is. Obviously this is much easier to do with closed holds than open holds. Just rotate the whole thing. This takes a little finesse. You want to get the yo moving and keep it out so the hold will keep its shape. Otherwise it all falls apart and you look like a fool. Unfortunately there's no real trick to it; just have to do it.

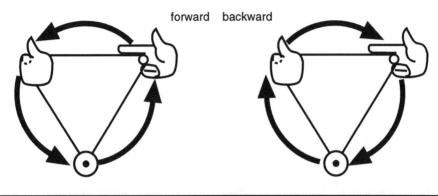

forward   backward

Sling

A sling is giving full rotation to a YT(4) hold. Not much to explain, get in a YT(4) and whip the thing around. If you haven't crossed up the string it should neatly throw out to a straight sleeper just by letting the string slide off your finger. (which makes it a good exit move)

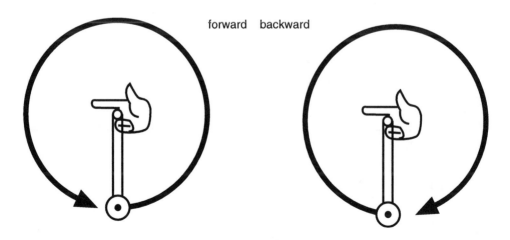

forward   backward

If you get to the phantom (20) hold, you can do it out of that one too.

Cradle

For a cradle, you have to be in an open hold that has the yo hanging, like FT(2), FTF(7), or YTFT(18); closed holds just don't work. First add a finger to the corner that doesn't have the yo dangling off it (in the FT example below, it's the free hand). Then pivot your hand around so your pointed at the yo. Open it up, lower it and rock the yo.

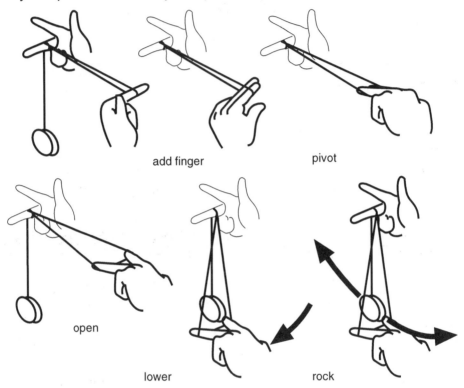

add finger · pivot

open

lower · rock

When you want out of the move, go out the way you came in (do it in reverse: raise, close, unpivot and remove a finger) and return to the hold you started with. If you get out of it other than how you got into it you're just begging for a knot.

If your hands aren't big enough or strong enough to use just 2 fingers, or if you just feel like a little variety, slide in more (or different) fingers then just pivot, open and rock like above.

freestyle style · kiddie style · heavy metal style

Pinwheeling is spinning the yo outside of the hold on the end seg. You can do this by either hooking the string with your finger or pinching it off. Obviously since this is a "miss" move you have to break plane to do it.

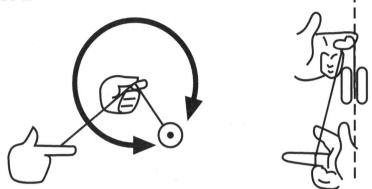

Pinching off the string is just that, pinching the string between your index finger and your thumb. For a hook, you just wrap your index finger around the string. Hooking the string is easier to do on the fly, but pinching the string is usually more precise and neater.

pinch   hook

What's funny is that often the plane breaking happens before the decision to pinwheel. That is that when you're trying to do a hit and you miss, if you're fast enough you can just hook or pinch and go into a pinwheel. And if you're a good enough liar, you can tell everyone looking at you that you meant to do it.

If the pinwheel is a move in the middle of the action or if you're trying to recover a miss, you'll have to get the yo back on the string, which means hitting the string out of a pinwheel: harder than it should be. Where the string comes into a pinch or hook is on a different plane than where it comes out. So you can't simply align the planes, you have to actually put the string in the path of the yo.

Around the World, ATW, is when you rotate a sleeper in a full circle. It's like a sling in a straight sleeper or a pinwheel with no pinch. To do it you need some kind of upward motion or lateral motion that you can turn into upward motion. If you want to go around the world by itself you'll get the motion from the throw but if you're doing this in action, you'll want some kind of launch move before it. Unravels, hops and loops are the most common moves that you can easily turn into an ATW.

If you're doing it solo, simply throw it out with a forward motion and cushion it at the end so you can get it to sleep then carry the yo through and around. If you're doing this midaction it's just going wide with a rotation and making sure it doesn't come back on you.

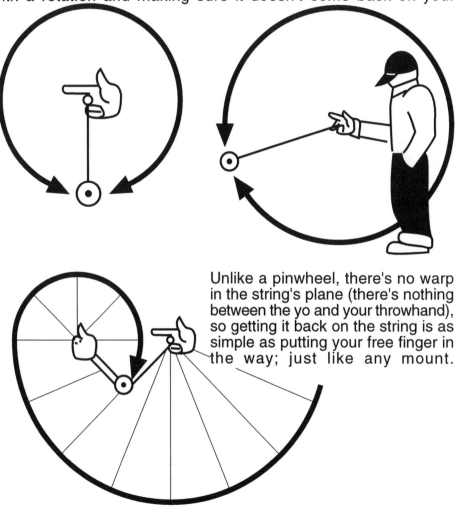

Unlike a pinwheel, there's no warp in the string's plane (there's nothing between the yo and your throwhand), so getting it back on the string is as simple as putting your free finger in the way; just like any mount.

The yo goes out and when it comes back instead of catching it you scoop your wrist around and throw it back out without it ever hitting your palm. Hard to explain, easy to understand.

One thing about loops, unlike any of the other moves, is that they aren't sleeper based, which means they are much easier to do on a fixed axle than a transaxle. Since transaxles have a habit of sleeping at the end of the string, the loop crumbles if you don't get the yo to catch real fast (and in midair).

Also a lot of Old Skool tricks are based on this move, which is one of the reason that Old Skoolers and Conquistayoers usually prefer fixed axles over transaxles. For most people it's easier to go New School with fixed axle than to go Old Skool with a transaxle.

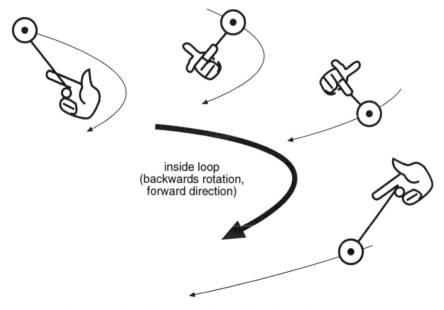

inside loop
(backwards rotation,
forward direction)

Loops can be done in either rotation direction, forward or backwards. In fact the rotation of a standard inside loop (the simplest, smoothest loop) is in fact backwards. The most common forward rotation loop is a "regeneration" and has a habit of shooting straight down (nature of the beast and gyrodynamics).

Another cool thing about loops is that they are the only move that allows you to put energy into the spin of the yo. In fact regenerations got their name from the technique of throwing in one in your freestyle action when the yo starts to slow down so you can keep going without stopping ("regenerate" the spin).

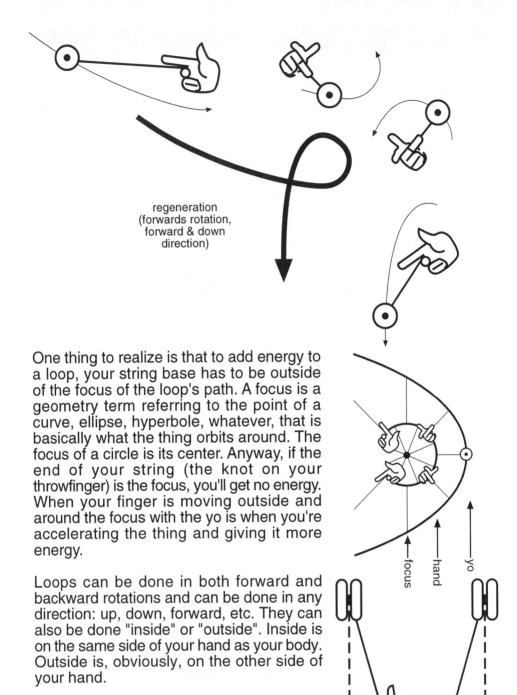

regeneration
(forwards rotation,
forward & down
direction)

One thing to realize is that to add energy to a loop, your string base has to be outside of the focus of the loop's path. A focus is a geometry term referring to the point of a curve, ellipse, hyperbole, whatever, that is basically what the thing orbits around. The focus of a circle is its center. Anyway, if the end of your string (the knot on your throwfinger) is the focus, you'll get no energy. When your finger is moving outside and around the focus with the yo is when you're accelerating the thing and giving it more energy.

Loops can be done in both forward and backward rotations and can be done in any direction: up, down, forward, etc. They can also be done "inside" or "outside". Inside is on the same side of your hand as your body. Outside is, obviously, on the other side of your hand.

Another thing to watch out for is inside loops loosen your string and outside loops tighten your string (opposite for lefties). This comes from the wind of the string. So if you're going for a record, double loop your string around your axle.

focus   hand   yo

inside   outside

Your exit is what you do to end up with the yo back in your hand. It's how you get out of the trick or refuel your action. A straight sleeper starts every action and it ends every action. Every exit takes you to a sleeper and the sleeper gets back to your hand.

Some tricks and moves end in a straight sleeper, so the exit is just jerking the yo back up.

Backtrack-The most conservative way is to just do whatever moves it takes to go backwards to a straight sleeper. For example if you end in a YF(3), then you'd tumble to a F(1) and free morph out; that's your exit. This is basically playing it safe. If you're in a formal contest usually you get points for just doing the trick and if you don't land it you get none. So you want to play it safe and not worry about being flashy.

Drop-The quick way out is dropping the trick. Just like the moves, you simply (and quickly) remove your fingers from the hold, letting the thing fall into a straight sleeper. If you don't have any crossed strings or mutations the thing should drop pretty clean. But this one does have the risk of knots and complications that backtracking doesn't, so be careful.

Throw out- The coolest way out is to throw the trick. You give the yo some outward motion and let it all go. The motion you'd use for a hop or just letting something like a pinwheel or a miss move carry through are the easiest way to throw out a trick. Throwing a "Rock the Baby" is a popular joke amongst 10 year old boys that find humor in the idea of hurting babies (and guys who write books about quantum physics and toys who find humor in the idea of hurting babies.--Hey, don't point your finger at me. "When the bough breaks, the cradle will fall..." is a pretty sick and twisted line if you ask me and I didn't come up with that one.)

Unravel- Like I said in its write up, unravel is a popular exit move and it ends in a straight sleeper. So another stylish exit is to plot a course to your nearest FYF(5) or YFYF(16) hold and let it rip.

String Break-an inconvenient way to end a trick, but potentially entertaining depending on where it flies.

Often loops are tacked on to the end of a trick to "puncuate" it (this is more popular with Old Skoolers). But since it's a zero move, you can call it part of the trick or part of the exit, it really doesn't matter.

V.
Holds

A hold is a triangular position of your fingers (plural), the yo and the string at any given time.

They are triangles for 3 reasons (to shut up the lawyers):
1) Two hands and one yo means that, mathematically, you can't have a square or a hexagon.
2) If we're talking real world math here, for three things (two hands and a yo) to not be in a triangle, they'd have to be in a straight line with zero deviation and until you can control your hands, the air and twitching of a spinning yo to absolute perfection, you won't get zero deviation.
3) Holds are things you move through. They are the turning points in a path. You can't change course in a three point straight-line without going through a triangle.

When we talked about quantum theory, I said that you can tell where one of these things is OR what it's doing. Holds are where something is. If you ever snap a picture of someone freestyling, the only thing you'll have is the hold the person was in when you hit the button. You don't get the action or the trick; a hold is just part of a trick not a trick itself.

Like I mentioned earlier, a cool thing about triangles is that you can stretch them and warp them and move them, but they always have the same three points. Here's an exercise, go get a penny, a nickel and a dime. Put them out on a table and picture a penny-nickel-dime (PND) triangle. Now move them around. No matter where you put them, you always have a penny-nickel-dime triangle. It may change direction, clockwise/counter clockwise, but no matter the shape, it's still PND (if you think you've got something else reread the first half of this).

Holds are the same way. At any given time, any position you find yourself in will be a certain TFY pattern and that triangle pattern is the hold.

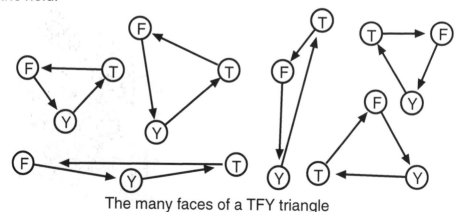

The many faces of a TFY triangle

Interpretting the Write Ups

This is the Micronesian tribal spirit that I put with the hold. (see the end of this chapter)

This is the TFY note for the hold

This is the number of the hold. It's just for reference.

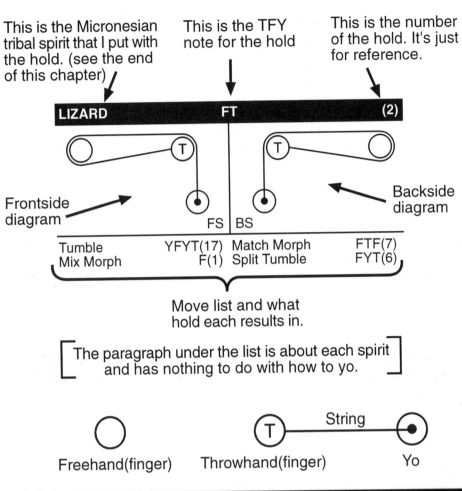

LIZARD   **FT**   **(2)**

Frontside diagram

Backside diagram

FS | BS

| Tumble | YFYT(17) | Match Morph | FTF(7) |
| Mix Morph | F(1) | Split Tumble | FYT(6) |

Move list and what hold each results in.

[The paragraph under the list is about each spirit and has nothing to do with how to yo.]

Freehand(finger)   Throwhand(finger)   String   Yo

The above diagram (FT) drawn out.

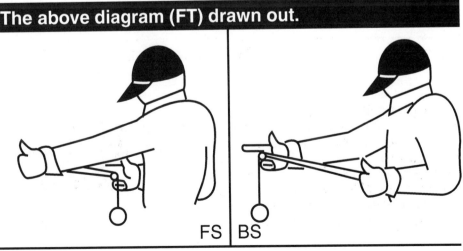

FS | BS

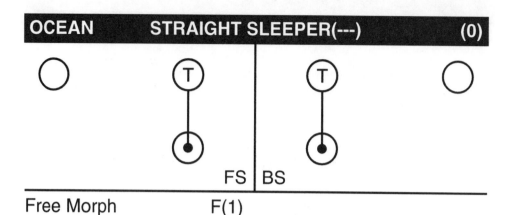

OCEAN   STRAIGHT SLEEPER(---)   (0)

FS | BS

Free Morph   F(1)

The Ocean is the spirit of the Straight sleeper because every trick and action has a sleeper in it just like the Ocean is believed to be the connecting force behind all life. This echoes the ideas of a grand oneness that you see in just about every major religion (and science when you realize that all living organisms still carry some form a saltwater in their biology).

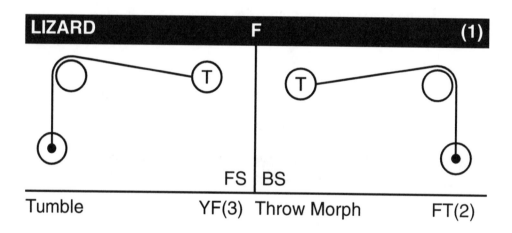

LIZARD   F   (1)

FS | BS

Tumble   YF(3)   Throw Morph   FT(2)

Although referred to as simply "The Lizard", our first spirit is more of a chameleon if you read the stories. He's the first spirit because he's the first lesson you learn in life: know your surroundings. This means not only "Don't throw ATW with someone behind you", but also know who your friends and family are, for better and worse.

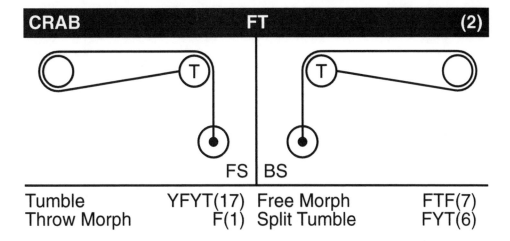

CRAB	FT		(2)
	FS	BS	
Tumble	YFYT(17)	Free Morph	FTF(7)
Throw Morph	F(1)	Split Tumble	FYT(6)

The Crab is second because he is the second lesson you learn in life. Once you know your surroundings you have to know yourself. The Crab has a hard shell and a big claw. The wisdom of The Crab is "stay true to yourself because when the chips are down you're the only one that can look our for you."

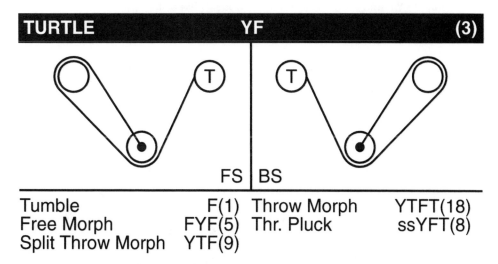

TURTLE	YF		(3)
	FS	BS	
Tumble	F(1)	Throw Morph	YTFT(18)
Free Morph	FYF(5)	Thr. Pluck	ssYFT(8)
Split Throw Morph	YTF(9)		

The Sea Turtle stories are all about enjoying what you have in life. A sea turtle swims casually around in the ocean, which (as we said before) is "life". The Sea Turtle spirit is said to just aimlessly enjoy swimming in life and teaches us to do the same. "Stop and smell the roses, while you can."

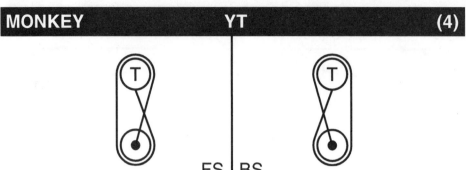

FS | BS

Free Pluck
A, Mix	YTF(9)
A, Match	ssFYFT(10)
B, Mix	FYTF(11)
B, Match	ssYFT(8)
C, Mix	FYT(6)
C, Match	ssYFTF(15)

Side + Freefinger move=Mix or Match

(ex:Frontside YT and a Forward Fr.finger move make a "Match"
Backside YT and a Forward Fr.finger move make a "Mix")

The fourth spirit is the Monkey. The Monkey is associated with YT because YT is the most unique (it's the only one with only 2 corners) and versatile hold and the stories of The Monkey teach us about the power of being original and versatile. The Monkey is always the character in a story that comes along and comes up with a solution to a seemingly unsolvable problem by thinking outside of what is expected. Often he gets laughed at, but in the end is right. The Monkey teaches us that thinking outside of what is expected is often "what it takes."

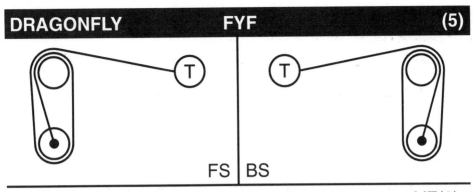

FS | BS

	FS		BS
Tumble	YFYF(16)	Free Morph	YF(3)
Thr. Pluck	ssFYTF(11)	Split Thr. Morph	FTYF(13)

The Dragonfly Spirit is confident and controls its fear. One story ends with the passage, "...And when you see a Dragonfly sitting atop a single reed, it is trying to remind you to have faith in the single thing and don't fear falling." Although this one applies to fear-not the knucklebiter nor contest anxiety, I think it best applies to life in general.

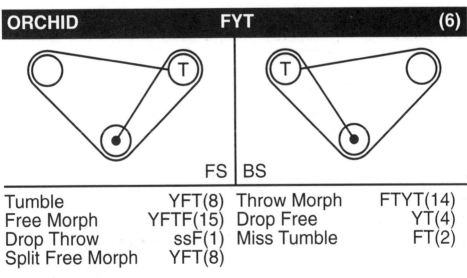

FS | BS

	FS		BS
Tumble	YFT(8)	Throw Morph	FTYT(14)
Free Morph	YFTF(15)	Drop Free	YT(4)
Drop Throw	ssF(1)	Miss Tumble	FT(2)
Split Free Morph	YFT(8)		

Funny thing: In these stories, orchids are considered animals and not plants like other flowers (a little trivia there for you). The Orchid Spirit has a strange role in her stories, she's always like the romantic interest but not completely. The best interpretation that I have is that the Orchid Spirit is the mysteries of life that we always want but never understand.

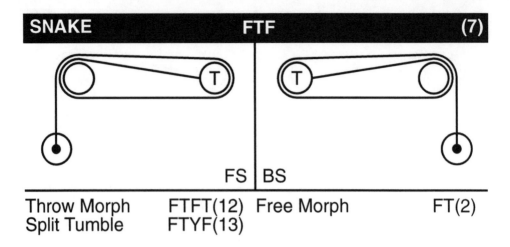

SNAKE		FTF		(7)

	FS	BS	
Throw Morph	FTFT(12)	Free Morph	FT(2)
Split Tumble	FTYF(13)		

The Snake Spirit is said to represent time. It can move very fast and very slow. It is cyclical and often repeats itself or returns to where it started. In fact, in any sanctified drawing or sculpture of the Snake Spirit it will be either in a coiled position or have an elaborate repeating pattern of scales. Inescapable symbolism there.

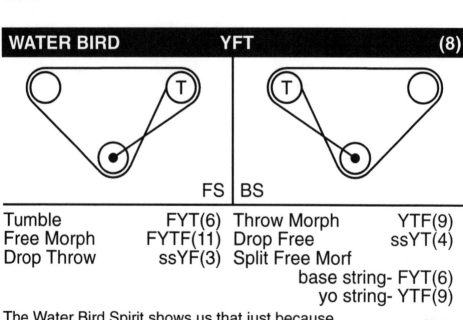

WATER BIRD		YFT		(8)

	FS	BS	
Tumble	FYT(6)	Throw Morph	YTF(9)
Free Morph	FYTF(11)	Drop Free	ssYT(4)
Drop Throw	ssYF(3)	Split Free Morf	
		base string-	FYT(6)
		yo string-	YTF(9)

The Water Bird Spirit shows us that just because you're around something doesn't mean you have to be like it. Think of it as I read it, "Ducks and sea gulls live on the water, but they are never wet." For yoing it reinforces the value of personal style, for living, it reminds us not to pick up our friends' bad habits.

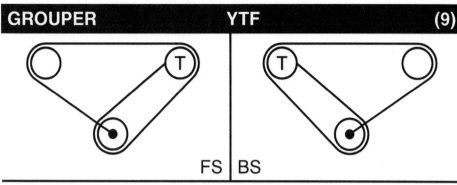

GROUPER   YTF   (9)

FS | BS

Tumble	YTYF(19)	Throw Morph	YFT(8)
Free Morph	FYFT(10)	Drop Free	YT(4)
Thr. Pluck	ssYTFT(18)	Split Free Morph	YFT(8)
Miss Throw Morph	YF(3)		

Groupers are big slow moving fish. The stories of the Grouper Spirit usually revolve around the idea of patience and stability. The Grouper is always the character that knows when the right time for something is.

CANOPY BIRD   FYFT   (10)

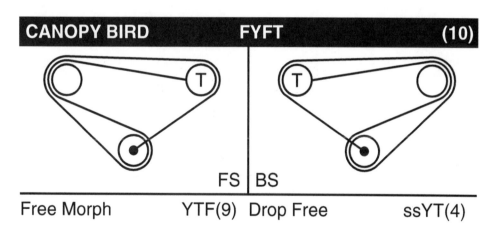

FS | BS

Free Morph	YTF(9)	Drop Free	ssYT(4)

The name "Canopy Bird" refers to a bird that lives up in the tree tops of the forest canopy (it's the way the translation works out). The Canopy Bird is said to always be watching you. It is up high and you can't see it but it's always there, observing and learning. And it'll tell you what you need to know, but you have to be listening for it.

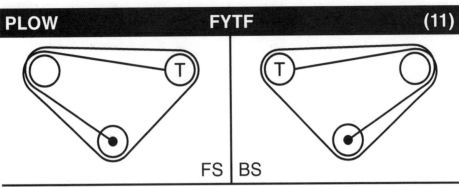

FS | BS

Free Morph	YFT(8)	Drop Free	YT(4)
Drop Throw	ssFYF(5)	Split Tumble	FTYF(13)

The Plow is the only nonliving spirit in the group. The theory is that it is the unnatural influence of man. The main lesson of The Plow is that material things often don't get rid of problems as much as they just give you a different set of them.

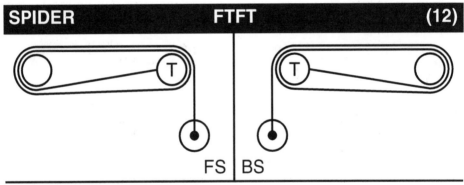

FS | BS

Throw Morph   FTF(7)

The Spider Spirit is the master of grace and balance. Not just physically but in its whole life. It knows that when you have many things happening at once you have to keep up and balance. Like a real spider, it has a huge web, but it is smooth and can walk around in it without getting stuck like everyone else because it's aware and walks lightly.

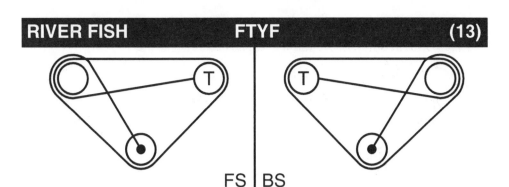

FS | BS

Split Tumble   FYTF(11)   Miss Tumble   FTF(7)
Miss Throw Morph   FYF(5)

In his stories, the River Fish Spirit is the guide through murky waters or dark places. Even though he's often doubted he holds true and comes through. The lessons are usually to the tune of, "Have faith", "Trust the opinion of the person that knows, " and "Don't cling so hard to your ways that you can't listen to someone else."

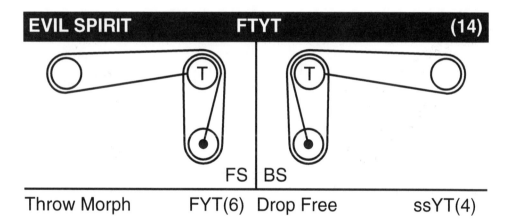

FS | BS

Throw Morph   FYT(6)   Drop Free   ssYT(4)

FTYT is a touchy hold so its spirit is the Evil Spirit. Interestingly though, the stories with the Evil Spirit usually don't have the "Bad things happen to bad people" theme that most of our Western stories do. Often the theme is "Bad things just happen". Which is a good point. Sometimes you'll just miss the trick and that's the way life goes.

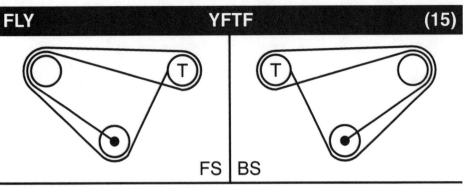

FS | BS

| Free Morph | FYT(6) | Drop Free | ssYT(4) |
| Drop Throw | ssYF(3) | | |

If you've ever tried to swat a fly you know how they always seem to be one step ahead. The lesson we get from the Fly Spirit stories is to always be prepared (maybe the Boy Scouts got that from the Fly Spirit). In throwing this means to always be thinking about what move or hold you're doing next. For real life it means stay prepared for anything and focused on your ultimate goal.

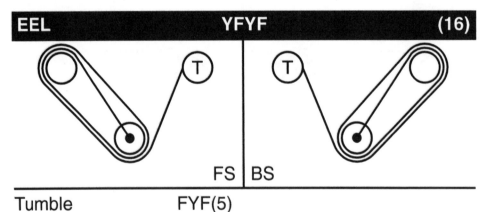

FS | BS

Tumble	FYF(5)

The Eel Spirit is a slick character that knows when to retreat into his rock. The big theme behind the Eel story (there's only one) is to know when to stay and when to cut your losses and duck out. A valuable skill for anyone throwing (in a grander sense, life) is to be able to tell when a trick is going bad so you can get out before you get a knot or clock yourself in the nose.

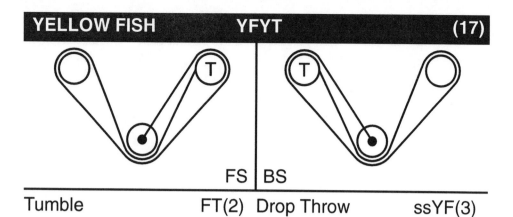

FS | BS

Tumble   FT(2)   Drop Throw   ssYF(3)

The Yellow Fish Spirit's stories are all about strength in numbers and the support you get from friends. The thing that I found interesting is that in the stories, Yellow Fish is always talked about as being in a school, but is written entirely singular.

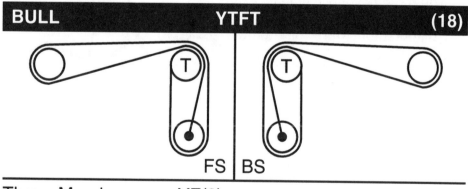

FS | BS

Throw Morph   YF(3)

The Bull Spirit is all about being tough. There's an updated phrasing of a passage in the second Bull story that I love, "Life's a bull, it tramples the weak while the strong compare scares over the bar-b-q." "Bar-b-q" was originally written as what roughly translates into, "grilled steak", which refers to the meat of life (but I just like to say "bar-b-q").

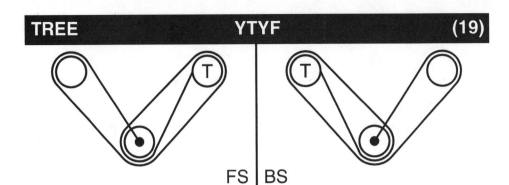

FS | BS

Tumble　　　　　YTF(9)

The Tree, which isn't considered an actual "spirit", is the connection of our world or life to the afterlife, which in these stories is the wild blue yonder. The symbolism is how a tree can carry the Ocean (that's "life", remember) as sap from the ground up to the skies. Another reason that it is the last in the order. There maybe more beyond it, but that's for another book, just like there's more to existence, but that's for another life.

Once upon a time, in a bookstore far away a poor writer dug through the bargain book section. Now as you may know, when a book doesn't sell they rip the cover off to send back to the distributor to show that the book is dead (like that whole Indian scalping thing with the British). Usually they then throw the book out, but there was this one bookstore by my house that would sell the coverless books for a dollar. And one day I found this book of tribal stories from somewhere in Micronesia (I liked the pictures). An old man had told these stories from his tribe's religion/tradition to the author, who then wrote them down. But the author could never figure out where the old man was from. It was a funny little story in the intro. I read it and thought it was pretty cool. Now I read a lot different philosophy and religion books and I could pick up on ideas in the morals that were like other books I'd read (not surprising when you realize that that area is where a lot of Oriental trade routes crossed a few hundred years ago) So I let one of my buddies who's also into that stuff borrow it. We then promptly forgot about it.

Flash forward 3 years. I'm working on this book and come up with these holds. Not one to leave huge spaces in a layout, I'm looking for a way to fill the voids. I figure I'll name the holds. I asked everyone if they could think of anything that there was 19 or 20 of. I got 12 days of Christmas, 12 signs in the Zodiac, 23 face cards in a tarot deck, 70-something bits in the I Ching, but no 19 or 20. Until I ask my buddy. He goes back to his closet and digs through a cardboard box that he never unpacked from the last apartment he lived in and produces this book. "The Mythology of a Micronesian Tribesman." Unfortunately the first 6 pages were either torn off with the cover or ripped off while being shuffled around in the bin of dead books many years earlier, so I never could figure out who wrote it (which sucks because I want to buy a good copy of it). But the stories held true (for life and yoing) and there were as many spirits as there were holds. It was a good match: 20 mathematical variations of a string triangle and 20 recurring characters in a series of fairy tales from the other side of the world.

VI.
Sidestyle

Sidestyle is throwing the yo so that the plane of the thing is parallel with your shoulders instead of perpendicular. For TFY transcription, sidestyle holds are noted with a "S" at the head. So a sidestyle frontside hold is noted "SFs." and a sidestyle backside hold is "SBs." All of the math still holds true, but there are some differences in the way things happen.

(side throw)

The first difference is that the yo faces a different direction. In/out and forward/backward are now left/right or to the free/throw. For this you have to throw the yo in a different direction: out to the side. No real difference other than when you cock your arm, face your elbow out to the side instead of forward.

There is also a difference between side mounts and regular mounts. Since regular forward action is more limited in space around the trick (your body is in line with the plane of the trick), you do regular mounts off of a hanging sleeper. That is, you throw a sleeper and then do the mount. Sidestyle doesn't have the space limitations, but it does have more limitations on your arm movement. Put these things together and it adds up to the fact that side mounts are done off of swinging sleepers instead of hanging sleepers. For this you want to throw out to the side so that as the yo is going out it will be going down and move into a swing. A good rule of thumb is to make sure the yo is all the way out by the time it swings through the bottom of the curve.

Throw

Swing

≈ 84 ≈

When it comes to actually moving the yo around, the biggest difference is that in sidestyle you don't have one hand coming conveniently in from each side of the plane. Both hands are on the same side of the plane and you have to worry about them crossing either each other or the plane.

One way to get around this is to get around the trick. "Hugging" the trick is when you reach one arm around or over the trick. It's called "hugging" because that's what it looks like you're doing to the trick, hugging it. When you hug a trick you don't have to worry about your hands getting crossed, but you do have to worry about the trick getting crossed with your arm. Your arm does cross the plane. Not a problem as long as the trick isn't too big. Small tricks can whiz around and never reach out to where they would hit the arm that is wrapping around. But if the trick gets big or you get sloppy, the yo will hit your arm and that will kill the whole thing.

hugging a trick

Since you don't start out with a trick in a hug, a hug can appear as a move. Which is simply wrapping your throw arm (I've never seen a free hug) around the trick. A good example would be: Overmount, Hug, Twist. An overmount (which I'll talk more about in a bit) is throwing a sleeper sideways and swinging it up and over your free finger into a SFs.YF(3) in front of you (as a trick it's the ever popular "Trapeze"). Then the "hug" would be shifting your throw hand out and around so that when you did the twist, it would be tucked into your throw arm. Hugging a trick has the same position for your arms as if you were holding a rifle at that height.

The alternative to having one arm cross the plane is to have one arm cross the other. In fact, when your throwing sidestyle, backside holds are ones where your arms are crossed. Frontside is when they're uncrossed. The problem is that normal humans can't cross their arms more than once in a direction. So if you do a single move in one direction, you have to do the next in the other direction since you can't continue in that direction because your arms won't wrap around that much and stay with the plane. For example, I'll start out in a SFs.YF(3) and do a free morph where my hands rotate to the left into a SBs. FYF(5). Remember to the left has replaced forward for describing the rotation. My next move needs rotate to the right, like another free morph or a tumble to the right. This is because to do another left rotation I'd have to cross my arms again. Which is very difficult for we normal humans to do without breaking plane.

A good way to deal with this is to do multi moves. With multi moves you can move through the tricky backside position real easy. And when you do moves like a hop or dunk, you can move through the backside hold without even moving your hands. Unfortunately the only lap you can do is a yo lap; free and throw laps double cross your arms. Unravels and exit moves are pretty much the same as with forward throws.

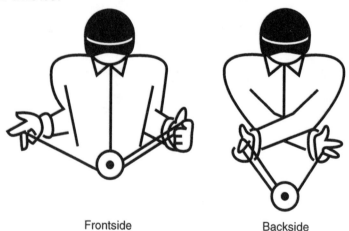

Frontside   Backside

Backside sidestyle is difficult and usually messy, but if done right can be good stuff. One uncomplicated way is to throw mounts backside. The easiest way to do this is to throw the yo, cross your arms and then swing it into the mount. Which arm you put on top will depend on the rotation of the move that you want to pull after you get the yo on the string. You'll just have to think ahead.

Over

Over mount is the most basic of side mounts. Throw a side sleeper into a swinging motion so you can get it up and over your free finger. Then simply keep the yo on the plane while it swings up and over your finger. The closer to the yo your freefinger is, the easier it is to get on the string (angular divergence). Although the further your yo is from your finger the cooler it looks. It leaves you with a SFs.YF(3).

The tension of the swinging yo will keep the string taught. Which is good, it's not easy to hit a slack string. So when the yo hits, move your throw hand in so the yo can sink into the string.

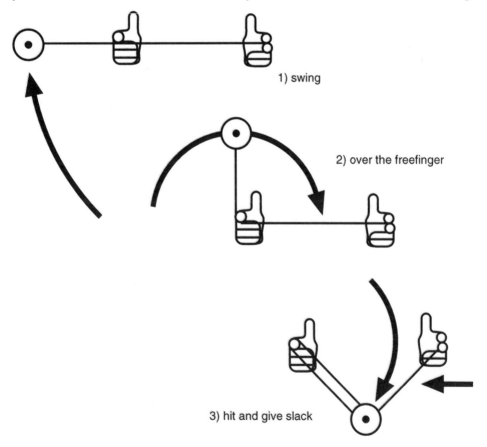

1) swing

2) over the freefinger

3) hit and give slack

This mount when done by itself for a trick is called "Trapeze" or "Man on the Trapeze" or something like that.

One and a Half

One and a half mounts start with a throw and a swing that has just enough momentum to get over your free finger but no more. When the yo reaches the top of its swing, put your freefinger in and hit the string on the underside. As the yo comes down swing it back, up, and over your throw finger. Let it swing over and give it slack when it hits the string. You'll end with a SFs.FYT(6).

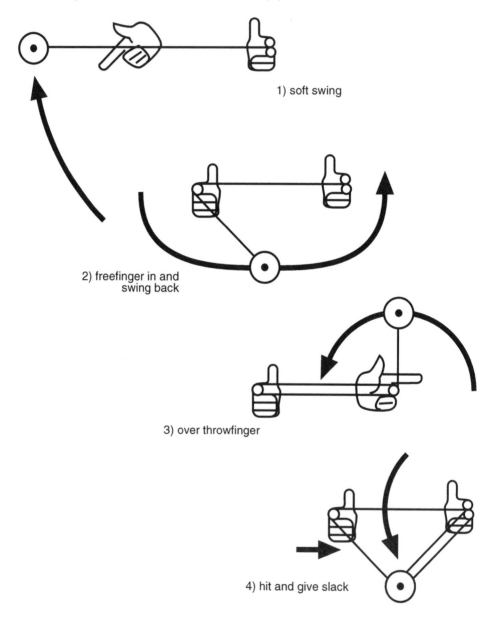

1) soft swing

2) freefinger in and
swing back

3) over throwfinger

4) hit and give slack

Doubles are just like overmounts, except you get a swing that is good enough to carry the yo over both hands then back around, over your free finger and down into a SFs.FTYF(13) (don't forget to give it slack when it hits).

Unlike regular forward double mounts, sidestyle doubles get their name from the fact that the yo goes around the hold twice before it's all over. As a trick this mount is called "Double or Nothing".

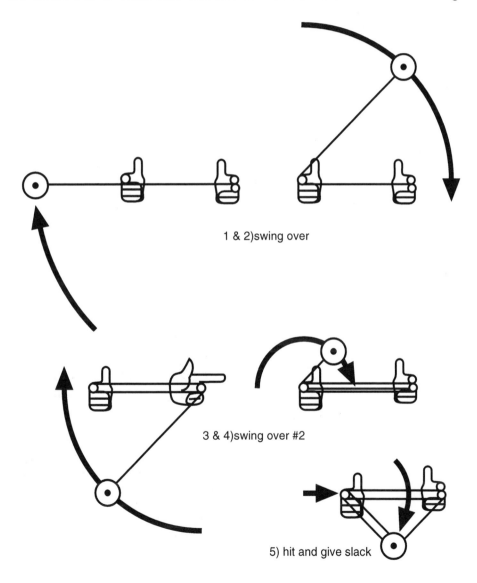

1 & 2)swing over

3 & 4)swing over #2

5) hit and give slack

Start with the same throw and soft swing from the one and a half that put the yo just over your free finger. When the yo reaches the top of its swing put your freefinger in and hit the string on the underside. As the yo comes up and into the string, give it a little slack from your throw hand and scoop your free finger under the yo. The yo should continue over and into a SFs.FYF(5).

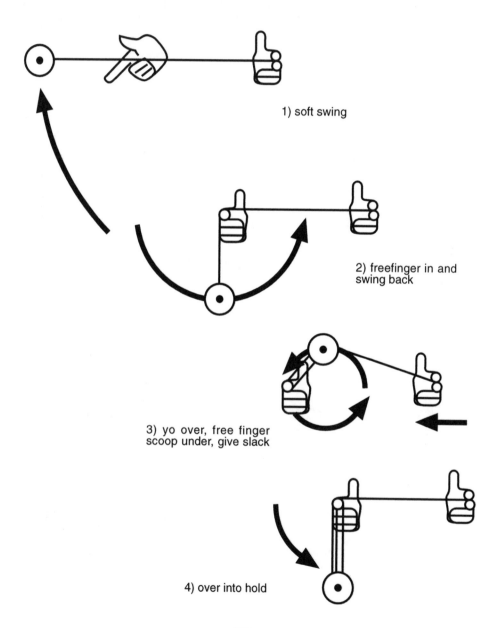

1) soft swing

2) freefinger in and swing back

3) yo over, free finger scoop under, give slack

4) over into hold

VII.
Tricks

A trick is a set of moves and the holds that go along with them. They're a predetermined path. Action is an unnamed (and often not predetermined) string of moves. If you have some action with a trick sandwiched in the middle, it's just that, "Action with a [whatever trick] in it". It's all a name game, but for the sake of definition (to shut the lawyers up) I'll say that a trick is a predetermined and named set of moves. And if that set of moves appears in a string of moves other than the trick's with a throw at the beginning and a landing at the end, then it's part of some action.

Freestyle tricks start with a mount of some kind. Mountless tricks are tricks that don't start with a mount, like Rock the Baby. Those write ups start with "Bs/Fs. Sleeper". If you want the full write up of a mount (starting with "Bs/Fs. Sleeper") they're at the end of the Mounts section.

Some tricks "Reset". A resetting trick is one where the series of moves leaves you back at a point where you can repeat it. These are tricks that can be done until you mess up, run out of string, or run out of spin. Reset patterns are marked with these bracket-like-thingies {}. {<--this is where the resetting part starts and when you get to the other one -->}, you go back to the -->{. That simple.

Some resetting patterns backtrack. So some of the moves are actually going backwards over the ones before them to drop you where you started. Other resetting tricks are circular. Those are ones that head in one direction and develop into something that happened earlier. These usually involve tumbles, since tumbles are direction neutral (forward tumbles give you the same thing a backward tumbles). The thing to watch out for with circular resetting tricks is since you're going continually in one direction you end up winding the string around your throw finger. This doesn't affect the moves or the holds as far as the trick is concerned, but it does mean that the string in the hold is getting shorter and your the trick is shrinking. So when you end the trick, just point your throw finger at the yo and let the winds fall off and get taken up. Real easy. Throw outs are good exit moves for circular tricks.

In this section I've drawn out 11 transcribed tricks to give you an idea of how it works. After those is a transcribed list of others (mostly variations of the 11) that I didn't bother drawing out. I tried to make that list as complete as I could, but I only have so much time, space and patience. The next section has some untranscribable tricks. Needless to say this is not the end-all listing of tricks, but it should be enough to keep you busy for a little while and give you some ideas so you can conjure up your own. Which, after all, is the point.

Bs.Sleeper (0), Free Morph (Back)-Fs.Y(1), Throw Morph (Back)-
Bs.FT(2), Cradle, Exit

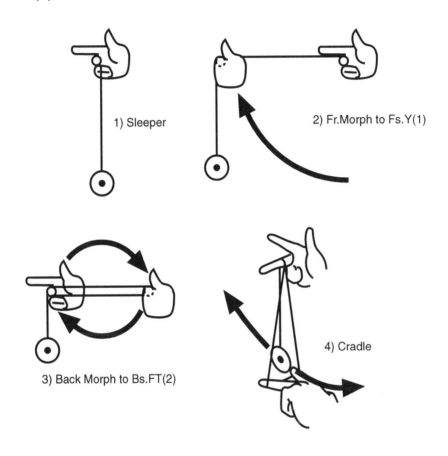

1) Sleeper

2) Fr.Morph to Fs.Y(1)

3) Back Morph to Bs.FT(2)

4) Cradle

This basic version is a mountless trick. It's all but a single move.
You get into a FT(2) real quick and cradle it. See the "Cradle" write
up in the Zero moves section for more info. For the first morph
(step 2), you want to pull the string 3/5 (just over a half) the way
up from the yo. For the second morph (step 3) you want to bend
the remaining string at a 1/3 of the way up from the yo. These are
the same points as with a top double mount so check that write
up for a drawing.

Front Top Single Mount-Bs.YF(3), {Backward Tumble-Fs.F(1), Backward Tumble-Bs.YF(3)}

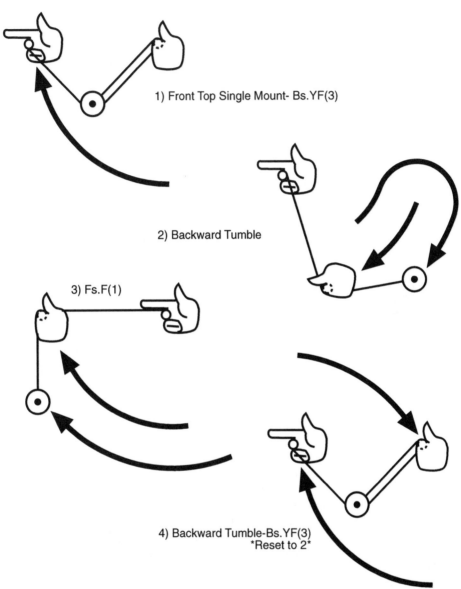

1) Front Top Single Mount- Bs.YF(3)

2) Backward Tumble

3) Fs.F(1)

4) Backward Tumble-Bs.YF(3)
Reset to 2

Sewing Machine got its name because it developed out of doing "Thread the Needle" and resting it. "Thread the Needle" is pretty much just a front top single mount and then tumbling out of it. For "Sewing Machine" don't tumble the thing all the way out, keep your free finger against the string and it'll reset real easy.

Back Top Single Mount-Fs.YF(3), Throw Pluck-Fs.YFT(8), Free Drop-Fs.YT(4), Backward Sling, Exit-Throw Out

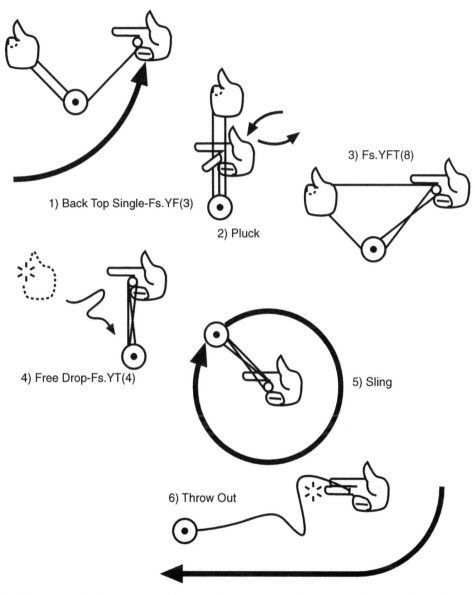

1) Back Top Single-Fs.YF(3)

2) Pluck

3) Fs.YFT(8)

4) Free Drop-Fs.YT(4)

5) Sling

6) Throw Out

This one is basically the quickest way into and out of a sling.

CAUTION: You can get a good bit of speed going in a sling... and then you let it go, so make sure you're out of range of anything that will break or punch you if you hit it.

Front Top Single Mount-Bs.YF(3), Forward Twist, Exit*

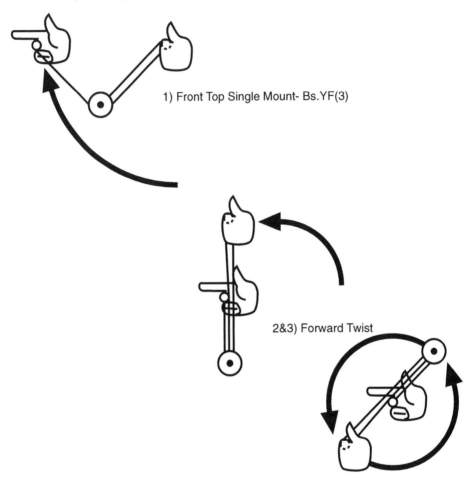

1) Front Top Single Mount- Bs.YF(3)

2&3) Forward Twist

This is the least complicated way to get into a Twist; that's all.

*Some sources (and thus some contests) have an Unravel for the Exit move. If you end up in that position (or you just want to unravel it), do a Free Morph from the YF(3) to a FYF(5) and unravel that.

Front Top Single Mount-Bs.YF(3), {Bottom Switch Stance-Fs.YF(3), Free Morph-Bs.FYF(5), Unravel--Switch Stance-Bs.Yf(3)}

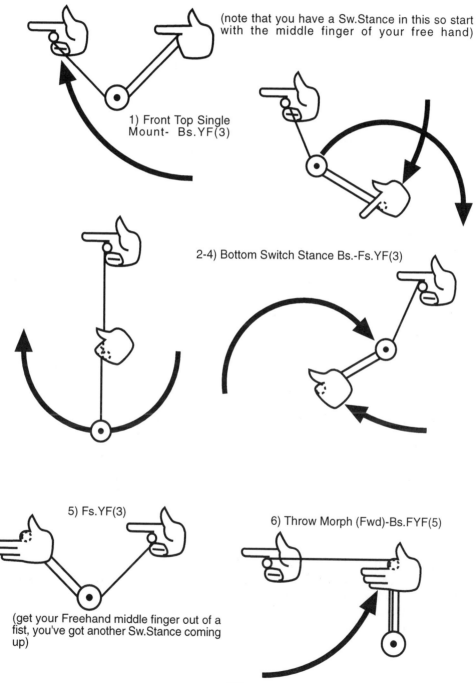

(note that you have a Sw.Stance in this so start with the middle finger of your free hand)

1) Front Top Single Mount- Bs.YF(3)

2-4) Bottom Switch Stance Bs.-Fs.YF(3)

5) Fs.YF(3)

(get your Freehand middle finger out of a fist, you've got another Sw.Stance coming up)

6) Throw Morph (Fwd)-Bs.FYF(5)

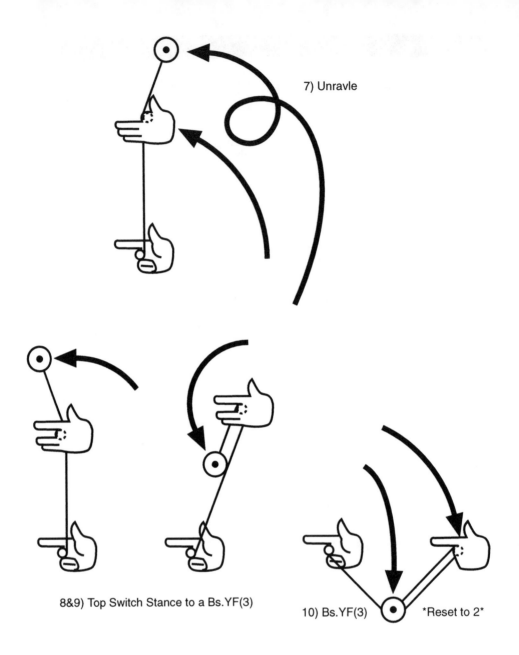

7) Unravle

8&9) Top Switch Stance to a Bs.YF(3)

10) Bs.YF(3)   *Reset to 2*

The Zipper (named for the carney ride) is another example of a resetting trick. The top Switch Stance (steps 8 & 9) leaves you with a Bs.YF(3) on your free middle finger (step 10), which is where you started with from the mount. So you can just start the trick over and keep going.

Front Top Split Mount-Fs.FYT(6), {Backward Tumble-Bs.YFT(8), Backward Tumble-Fs.FYT(6)}

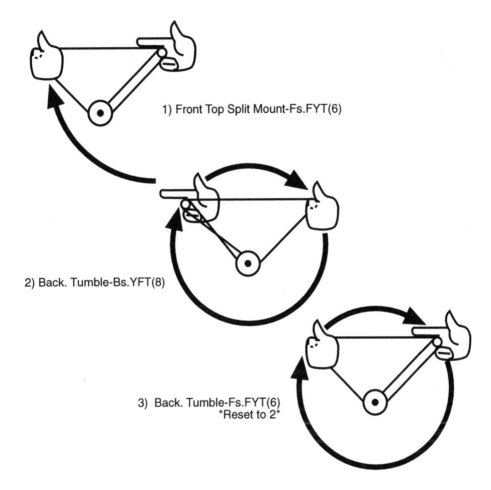

1) Front Top Split Mount-Fs.FYT(6)

2) Back. Tumble-Bs.YFT(8)

3) Back. Tumble-Fs.FYT(6)
Reset to 2

Like a Sewing Machine and an Overlock (Sewing machine variation), a Barrel Roll is just repeated tumbles. Since tumbles are direction neutral, you can keep going in one direction and it resets itself every other hold. This may be a resetting trick, but it's a circular one; so you end up with the string winding around your throw finger as you do it and since it's made up of two 4 seg holds, you feel it more than with the other repeating tumble tricks. This doesn't affect the moves, but it does mean that the trick is going to get progressively smaller as you go. If you don't mess up, the trick will end when the thing shrinks so small the yo hits your finger.

Over mount-SFs.YF(3), Throw Pluck-SFs.YFT(8), Throw Hop-SFs.FTYF(13), Throw Dunk, SFs.YFT(8), Exit

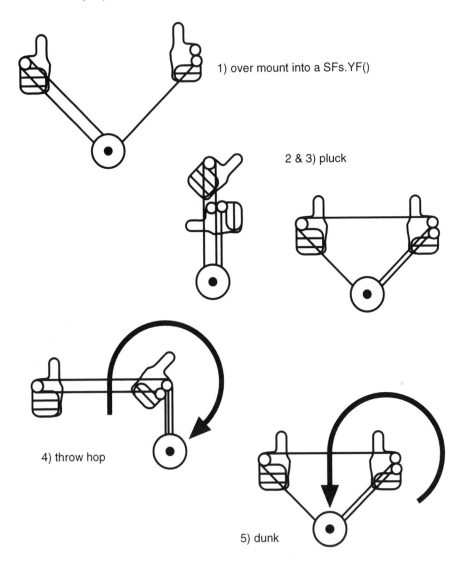

1) over mount into a SFs.YF()

2 & 3) pluck

4) throw hop

5) dunk

I like to do the pluck with my index finger (and so I drew it that way); it makes the hop and dunk a little easier although it's completely a matter of taste.

Front Top Single Mount-Bs.YF(3), Throw Pluck-Bs.YFT(8), {Throw Hop (Forward)-Bs.FTYT(14), Throw Morph (Forward)-Fs.FYT(6), Backwards Tumble-Bs.YFT(8)}

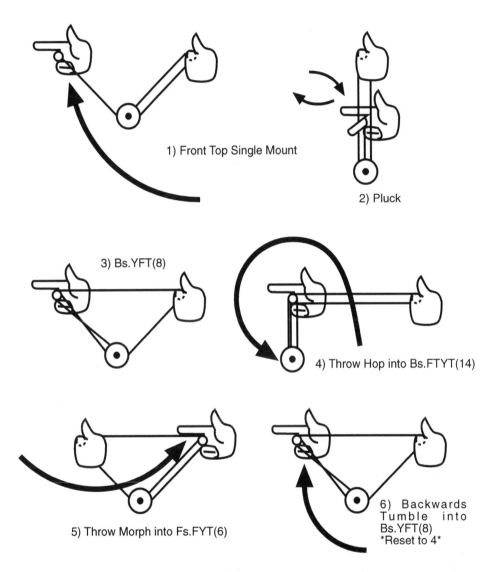

1) Front Top Single Mount

2) Pluck

3) Bs.YFT(8)

4) Throw Hop into Bs.FTYT(14)

5) Throw Morph into Fs.FYT(6)

6) Backwards Tumble into Bs.YFT(8) *Reset to 4*

This too is a resetting trick, but since it's not a circular one, the string doesn't wind around your finger. Often the last Morph/Tumble combo (5 & 6) will blend into a Throw Overscoop. It doesn't really matter if you tighten up into a Scoop or keep it loose, it's the same trick.

Back Top Single Mount-Fs.YF(3), Backwards Twist (1), Free Dunk (Backward)-Fs.YFYF(16), Free Morph-Bs.FYFYF, Unravle

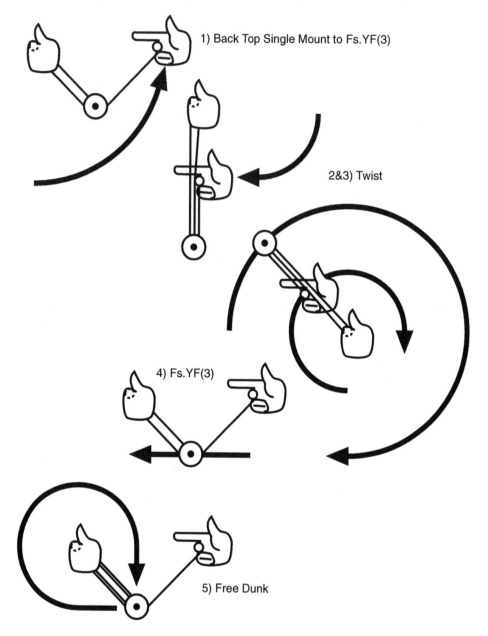

1) Back Top Single Mount to Fs.YF(3)

2&3) Twist

4) Fs.YF(3)

5) Free Dunk

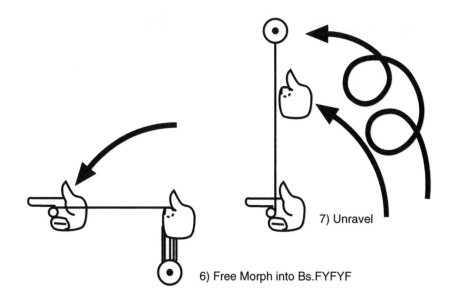

7) Unravel

6) Free Morph into Bs.FYFYF

For this trick it is significantly easier and smoother to pivot the Twist around the top (free) finger. The twist rolls smoothly out into the dunk when you do it right; basically you stop your fingers and the yo keeps going; out, up and over.

Another thing to notice is that Dunking a YFYF(16) gives you a 6 seg hold (FYFYF). This hold is one that you should move straight through. Do it fast, but realize that the Dunk and then this 6 seg hold are what make this trick tricky.

Front Top Single Mount-Bs.YF(3), Throw Pluck-Bs.YFT(8), Throw Hop(Forward)-Bs.FTYT(14), Forward Free Lap-Bs.YFT(8), Free Morph (Backward)-Fs.FYTF(11), Backward Tumble-Bs.YFYTF, Throw Drop-Bs.YFYF(16), Unravel

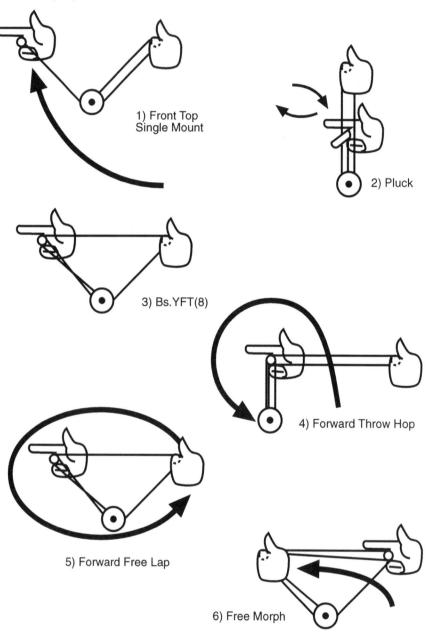

1) Front Top Single Mount

2) Pluck

3) Bs.YFT(8)

4) Forward Throw Hop

5) Forward Free Lap

6) Free Morph

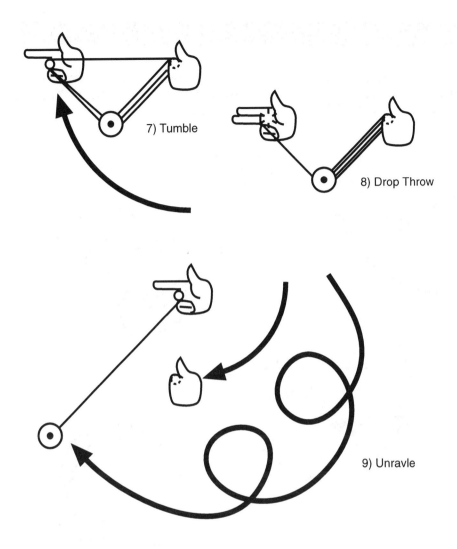

7) Tumble

8) Drop Throw

9) Unravle

When you do this trick quick and smooth, the Lap and Free Morph (steps 5 & 6) can blend smoothly into a single move of your finger. It's a little easier and a lot better looking.

Back Bottom Split Mount-Fs.FYT(6), Free Underscoop-Fs.FYTF(11), Backward Tumble-Bs.YFYTF, Forward Roll, Drop Throw-Bs.YFYF(16), Forward Tumble-Fs.FYF(5), Unravle, Loop

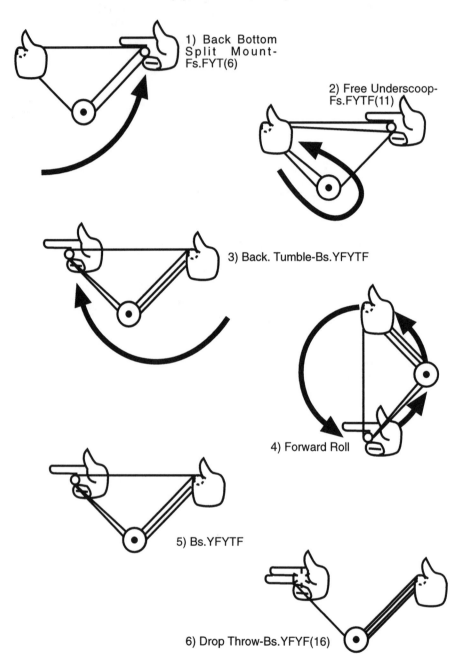

1) Back Bottom Split Mount- Fs.FYT(6)

2) Free Underscoop- Fs.FYTF(11)

3) Back. Tumble-Bs.YFYTF

4) Forward Roll

5) Bs.YFYTF

6) Drop Throw-Bs.YFYF(16)

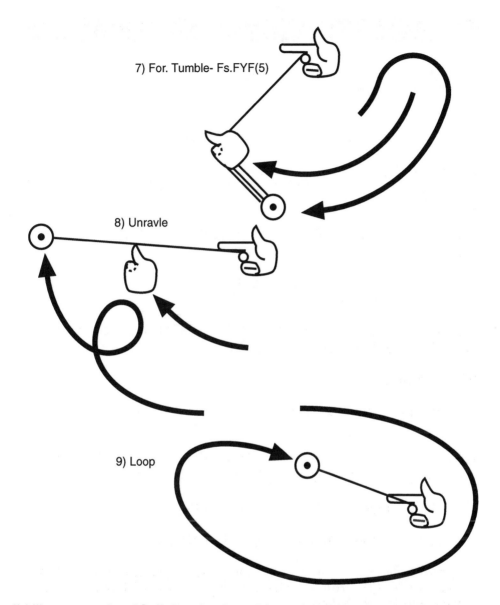

7) For. Tumble- Fs.FYF(5)

8) Unravle

9) Loop

I'd like to say that "Splitting the Atom" is a trick that has more versions and incarnations than I can count. Every source I've seen has a different version and Old Masters I've talked to have made references to "The *Old* Split the Atom". The version here is the one that I've always done, the one that was taught to me by one of my buddies that he personally got from one of the Old Masters. Although I have to admit, I usually don't bother with the end loop.

The forward tumble and the unravel (steps 7 & 8) will blend. In fact the reason the morph is in there, instead of just a straight unravel (like in Plan 9) is so you can get the yo going out for the loop.

Baby Wrap- Front bottom single mount-Fs.YF(3), Throw Morph (back)-Bs.YTFT(18), Cradle, Exit

Cat's Cradle- Bs.Sleeper, Free Morph (back)-Fs.F(1), Throw Morph (back)-Bs.FT(2), Free Morph (back)-Fs.FTF(7), Cradle, Exit

Mouse Cradle- Bs.Sleeper, Free Morph (back)-Fs.F(1), Throw Morph (back)-Bs.FT(2), Free Morph (back)-Fs.FTF(7), Throw Morph (back), Bs.FTFT(12), Cradle, Exit

Neuron Twister- Front Top Double Mount- Fs.YFYT(17), Forward Twist, Exit

Schizo- Front Bottom Single Mount-Fs.YF(3), Free Morph (for)-Bs. FYF(5), Forward Twist, Unravel

Overlock- Front Top Double Mount- Fs.YFYT(17), {Back Tumble-Bs.F(2), Back Tumble-Fs.YFYT(17)}

Walk the Dog-Sleeper, Grind (ground), Exit

Pinwheel (as a trick)- Bs.Sleeper, Free morph (Back)-Fs.F(1), Pinwheel, Exit

Caterpillar-Front Bottom Single Mount- Fs.YF(3), Free Overscoop-Fs.YFYF(16), Free morph (for)-Bs.FYFYF, Unravel

Warp Drive- {Inside Loop, Around theWorld}

Thread the needle-Front top single-Bs.YF(3), Exit

Zipper ala Bill-Front Top Single Mount-Bs.YF(3), {Bottom Switch Stance-Fs.YF(3), Free Morph-Bs.FYF(5), Forward Twist,Unravel--Switch Stance-Bs.Yf(3)}

Skin the Cat (alt.Tidal Wave)-Bs.Sleeper, Free Morph-Fs.F(1)(note: start freefinger at base of string, then slide out the string to a Fs.F(1) with a very short end layer then move smoothly into a...), Loop

Atom Smasher- variation of Split the Atom that I can't get a definitive source on.

Hydrogen Bomb-Again, a variation of Split the Atom that I can't get a witness on.

VIII.
Untranscribables

Untranscribables

As anyone who has ever tried to go dutch with more than 3 people at a restaurant after 1 AM can tell you, the world is not always mathematically correct. Yoing is no exception. QYT is designed to account for action that has some relationship to a plane. But if you choose you can show complete disregard for planes and math and quantums and just see what you can get the yo to do.

These are the untranscribables. The tricks that live outside the realms of trigonometry, where the only thing that matters is a spinning yo, string and a clean pair of underwear.

Old Skool started long before transaxles and QYT. So they are usually more fond of these tricks than New Schoolers.

To do a flying saucer you throw the yo down at a 45° angle and let it go into a flat spin. Hook the string just under the knot and pull it out, running your freehand down the string. This will shrink the part of the string which is flailing and spinning. You want to be raising your freehand as you pull it out so that by the time you get about 6 to 8 inches from the yo, your throwhand is level with the yo. Then let it go, give it a little tug and pop it back.

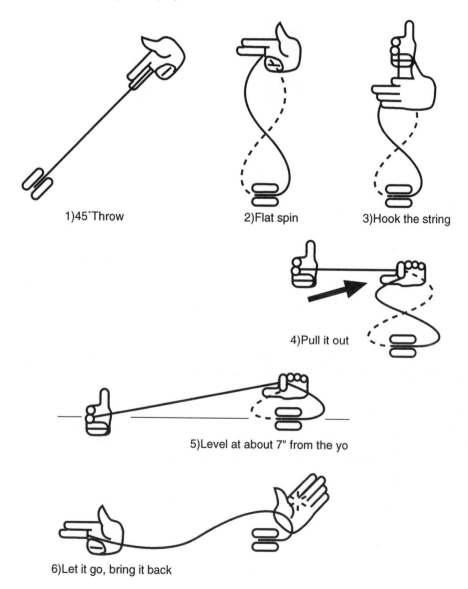

1)45°Throw

2)Flat spin

3)Hook the string

4)Pull it out

5)Level at about 7" from the yo

6)Let it go, bring it back

The cool thing about Flying Saucer is that when you're in the flat spin, the string is twisting and that either tightens or loosens the string. If you throw the yo to the right, it will tighten the string. If you throw it to the left, it will loosen the string.

Right=Tight

Left=Loose

No matter which way you throw it, after it's down it should go into the flat spin and you can hook the string and pull it out the same way. Nothing changes. The only difference is whether your string is looser or tighter at the end.

Needless to say, this fact makes Flying Saucer a popular move because it lets you tighten or loosen your string without having to kill your yo. So when your string tightens up from a lot of straight throws or if you want to shift from loop stuff to freestyle stuff, this is a quick and easy (and stylish) way to do it.

Lasso

Lasso is the same as Flying saucer, just without drawing out the string. It's a little trickier because you have to get the yo up to string level with a pull, but if you do it too hard you'll kill the spin. So use just enough pull to get it as high as you need and move your hand over and down to make it easier.

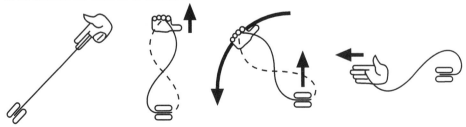

Skyrocket is done out of a sleeper. Take the knot off your finger so you're holding it. Pull the yo back up and when it hits your hand (or just before it) let it go so it flies up into the wild blue yonder.

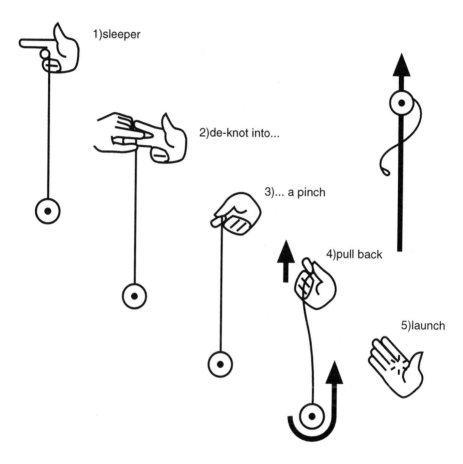

1)sleeper

2)de-knot into...

3)... a pinch

4)pull back

5)launch

Sky rocket is a move that you can tack onto the end of some action for a flashy end, like using a loop for punctation. But since you have to get back to a sleeper to do it, you still have to "exit" the trick first.

One thing to realize is that the more spin you have the higher it's going. So if you wait until the end of the action there may only be enough spin left to get it as high as your shoulder.

A flashy Old Skool thing to do after a skyrocket is to catch the yo somewhere showy. The easiest is to pull off your hat and catch it with that. Another one is to make sure your shirt's tucked in and catch it in your collar; that one's not too hard and you'll have a shirt on more often than you'll have a hat, pockets or elastic pants.

A move more popular with Fiends is to do a Skyrocket "air-to-surface". This is when you throw a sleeper and pull the knot off like usual, but then you swing it back and pull it up while it's swung back at an angle. When you do this the yo comes back at an angle and launches out instead of just up.

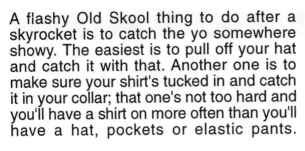

pocket
shirt pocket
hat
shirt (collar)
pants

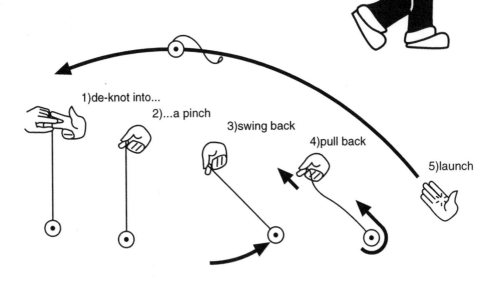

1)de-knot into...
2)...a pinch
3)swing back
4)pull back
5)launch

WARNING: This is another flying piece of plastic trick so be careful where you shoot it. Do this outside. Another thing to watch out for is that YOU will be in front of the yo when it goes, so be careful don't hit yourself with the yo when you pull it in.

Moon Rocket is a souped-up version of Skyrocket. Sidestyle: throw an over mount. Then take the string off both of your fingers so you have it pinched in both hands. Jerk your hands apart so the yo is shot up, letting go as soon as it's moving.

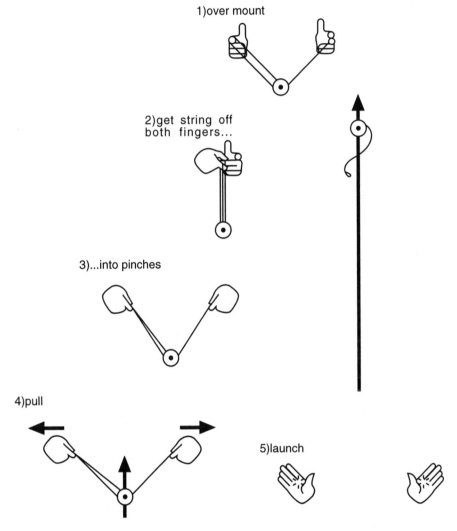

1)over mount

2)get string off both fingers...

3)...into pinches

4)pull

5)launch

Moon rockets can fly much higher than sky rockets. This is because the energy for a sky rocket comes from the spin of the yo, where as with a moonrocket, the energy comes from your arms.

Another deadly thing to look out for is air-to-surface moonrockets. I'll let you figure it out, but be warned, they have all the hazards of a/s sky rockets with much more power.

Start with a front top single mount. Then open your hands and fold them together like you were trying to shake hands with yourself. Jerk the yo up so it grabs all three segs in the wind and rolls up into your hands. Hold it for however long. Pull your throwhand down and back (like your starting up a lawn mower). The yo should pop out spinning, leaving you in a Fs.F(2).

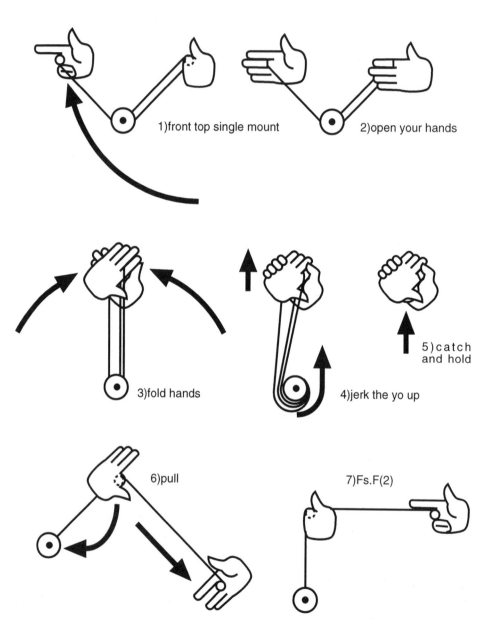

1)front top single mount

2)open your hands

3)fold hands

4)jerk the yo up

5)catch and hold

6)pull

7)Fs.F(2)

Drop in the Bucket

Sidestyle, lay out the string across the palm of your freehand about six inches from the yo. Point your thumb and index finger up and wrap the string round them, thumb first (that's clockwise if you throw with your right, counterclockwise if you throw with your left). Pinch the string with your free index against your middle finger. Get your throw finger in the loop around your free thumb and pull it out, releasing the string from between the index/middle pinch as you do. Swing the yo over and onto the center seg that should be lined up with the yo. Exit the way you came in.

(seen from above)

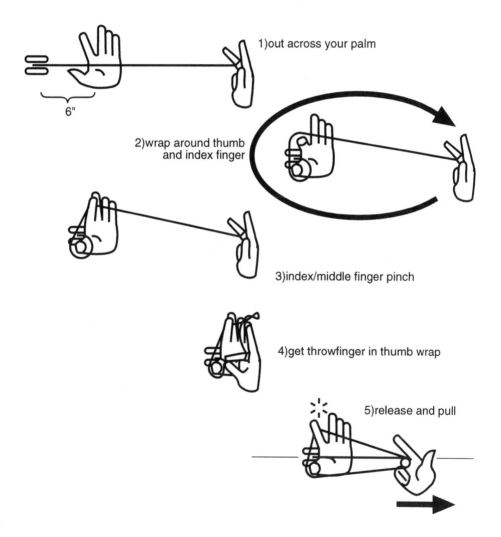

6"

1)out across your palm

2)wrap around thumb and index finger

3)index/middle finger pinch

4)get throwfinger in thumb wrap

5)release and pull

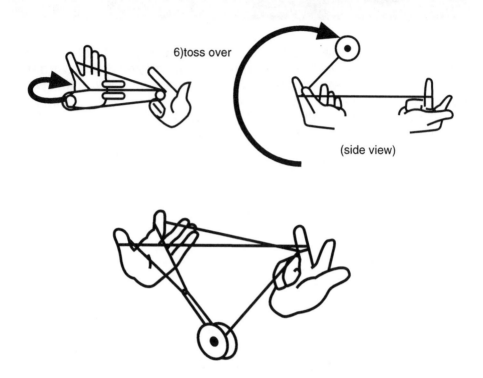

6)toss over

(side view)

After you wrap the string around your thumb and index finger, you pinch it with your index and middle finger, like crossing your fingers. This is so when you reach in to hook the wrap around your thumb, the string slacks between your hands instead of lowering the yo. You release the string so when you pull the loop back you're taking up the slack from the seg between your throwfinger and free index finger. This is easier than having the yo raise and lower because there's no tension on the string from the weight of the yo and thus less friction. So it's easier on your hand, easier to do, and you don't have to worry about the string sliding out of position.

And on a final note I'd like to say that without hesitation this is the most and ugliest knot-prone trick in this book. You've been warned.

As part of a trick, a "loop" is a zero move that can take many different shapes. And on their own, each of these can be a trick. I'm not going to bother giving full write up to all of the different variations, but here's a handful of the more popular ones.

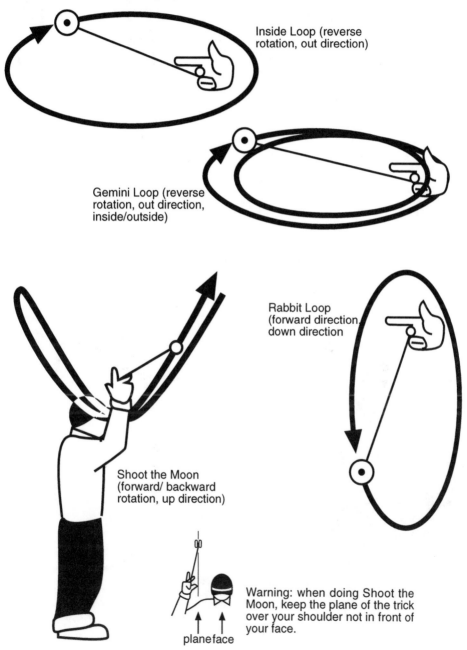

Inside Loop (reverse rotation, out direction)

Gemini Loop (reverse rotation, out direction, inside/outside)

Rabbit Loop (forward direction, down direction

Shoot the Moon (forward/ backward rotation, up direction)

Warning: when doing Shoot the Moon, keep the plane of the trick over your shoulder not in front of your face.

plane face

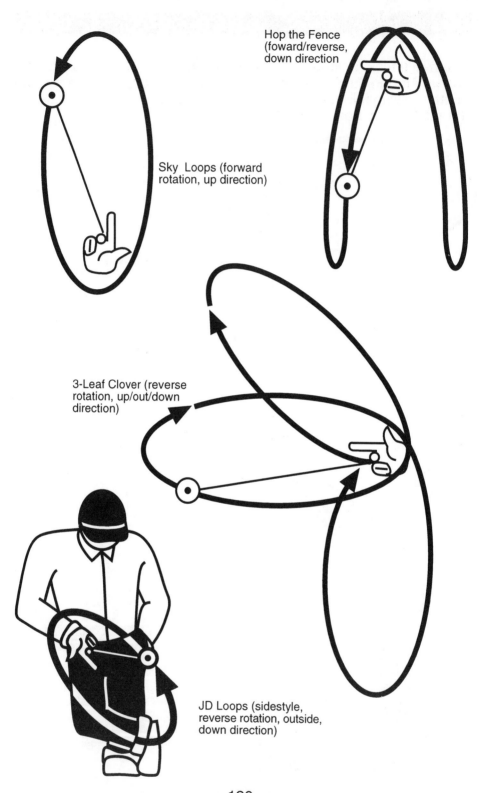

Hop the Fence
(foward/reverse,
down direction

Sky Loops (forward
rotation, up direction)

3-Leaf Clover (reverse
rotation, up/out/down
direction)

JD Loops (sidestyle,
reverse rotation, outside,
down direction)

Picture tricks are tricks where the string forms some kind of shape during a long sleeper. Here are a few of the more popular ones.

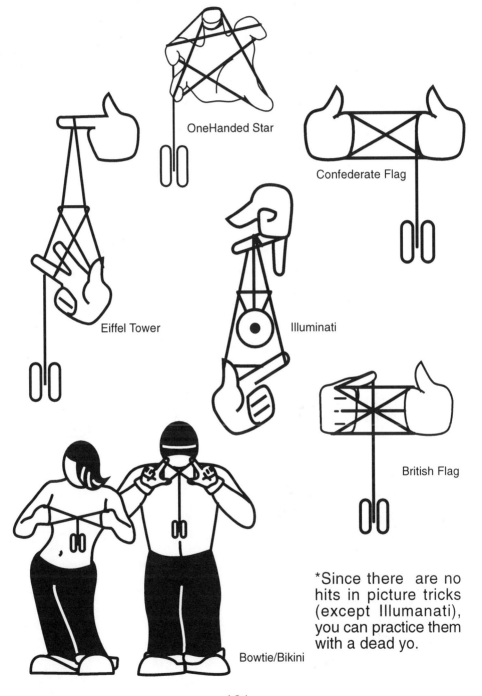

OneHanded Star

Confederate Flag

Eiffel Tower

Illuminati

British Flag

Bowtie/Bikini

*Since there are no hits in picture tricks (except Illumanati), you can practice them with a dead yo.

A Houdini Drop is a way to do a double mount into a SFs.YF(3)... or so it would seem. You throw a double mount. On the first pass, the string should bend around your index finger. Then put your middle finger out so the second pass can bend around that. After the second pass, as the yo hits the string, release the string wrapped around your index finger (the first pass). The yo will take up the slack as it sinks into the string (you can help it by pulling your hands apart). If you do it smooth enough, dropping the index finger wrap goes unnoticed by the common observer and it looks like you went straight into the hold.

A Houdini Drop is a sleight-of-hand trick, which makes it kind of cool. It's also and excellent example of using more than just your throw finger and one free finger.

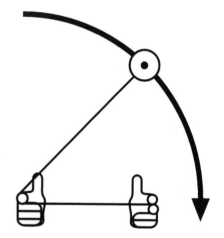

1&2) first pass on a double mount around index finger

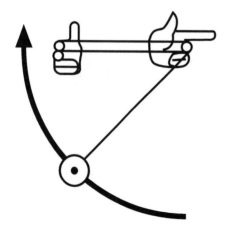

3)second pass around middle finger

4)hit second pass segment, drop index finger

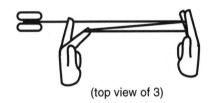

(top view of 3)

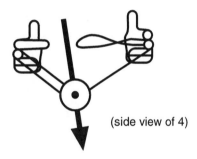

(side view of 4)

5)SFs.YF(3)

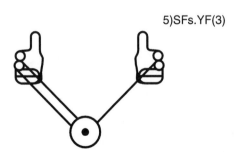

Another showy, magicy trick is an Oliver Twist. It's "magicy" because it doesn't look like it should work the way it does. Start with a SFs.YF(3) hold (an overmount will give you that) and hug it. Then do a double miss reverse yo lap. That is a yo lap where you miss both fingers as the yo passes with the string. For a little showmanship, have the yo come as close to, but outside of, your throw hand when it comes back around (it makes the trick look more impossible).

This trick works by moving into a mutation and then quickly out of it via a different route. Doing the first half of the lap, a miss free morph out of a SFs.YF(3), gives you a mutant SBs.YF(3) (the string is wrapped around the axle while the hold is upside down). Then as you complete the lap with a miss throw morph out of the mutant SBs.YF(3), the string unwraps and leaves you with the nice healthy SFs.YF(3) that you started with.

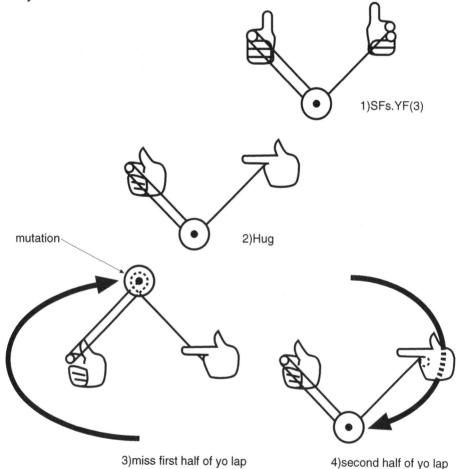

1)SFs.YF(3)

2)Hug

mutation

3)miss first half of yo lap

4)second half of yo lap

A Venus Finger Trap, like a Houdini Drop, is a trick that plays with extra fingers and dropping the string mid-move. This trick can be done without the use of the extra finger (the throw index), but that can be more difficult and often not as smooth. Start with a front top single mount. Pluck the string with the index finger of your throw hand. You should end up in a Fs.YFT(8), with the "T" corner around your index finger. Reverse tumble into a Bs.FYT (6). Then do another reverse tumble, but this time, as the yo is in mid air transfer to the base segment (backside), drop the wrap around your throw index finger. This might take a little finesse since by this point the string will be wrapped under your middle finger, around your index finger and then back under you middle finger. But that's where it gets its name. The tumble should continue into a Bs.YF(3); from their reverse tumble/unravel it.

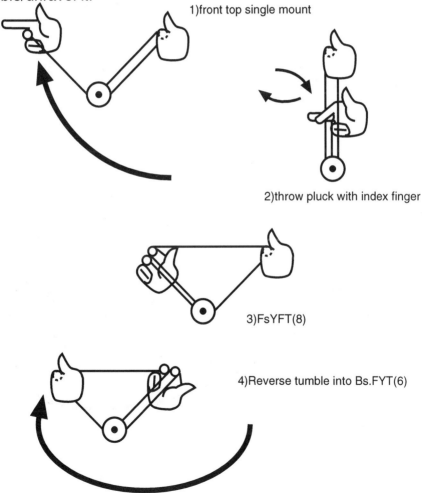

1)front top single mount

2)throw pluck with index finger

3)FsYFT(8)

4)Reverse tumble into Bs.FYT(6)

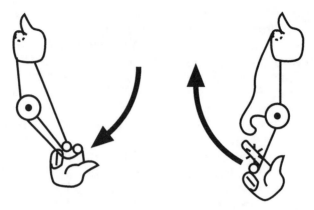

5)first half of reverse tumble

6)throw index drop and
second half of tumble

7)Bs.YF(3)

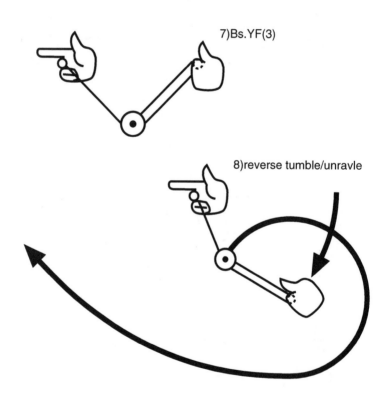

8)reverse tumble/unravle

An Arm Band is a good example of using a non-finger for a corner. In this case, it's your biceps. Throw an around the world out with a forward in rotation (this is the direction opposite of the usual ATW). Then keep your arm out and your shoulder square so your arm crosses the plane. As the yo swings back and around, it will hit your biceps and bend around it. If you've kept the plane straight, you should be able to catch it on the string stretching from your throw hand to the underside of your arm.

What makes this trick hard is throwing the yo and then resetting your arm into position while keeping the plane intact. So pay attention to keeping the plane straight.

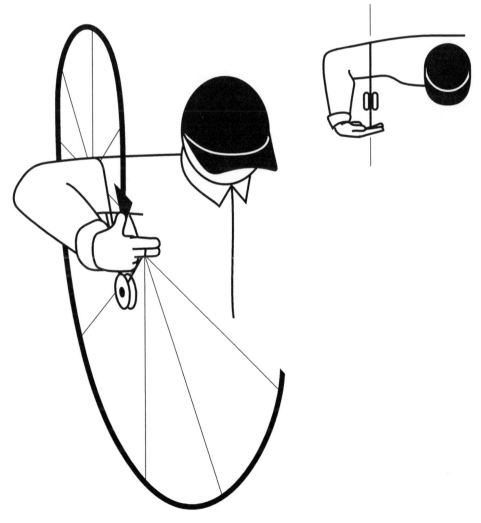

IX.
Other Stuff

...because there's more to do with a yo than tricks.

Dog Racing

Dog racing is real simple. Set up 2 lines with flat smooth ground between them (about 5 yards apart is good). Everyone who's in stands at one line. The ref calls, "Go", everyone throws a Walk the Dog then takes it off their finger and lets it go. The yos run and who's ever crosses the finish line first wins.

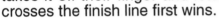

To add a little variety, add some obstacles like chutes, moguls and ramps. All you need is some duct tape and posterboard. But realize that if you make them too steep you won't be able to get over them.

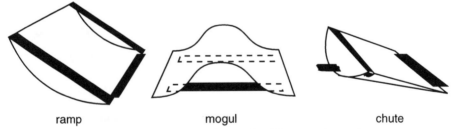

| ramp | mogul | chute |

Ramp- Curve a piece of posterboard with 2 strips of tape wrapped around opposite edges of the board and then tape one edge to the ground.

Mogul- Use two strips of tape to curve a piece of posterboard. But unlike with a ramp don't put it around the edges, tape them flat to the underside about 4 inches from the edge.

Chute- Curve one edge by taping around the other 2. Then tape the opposite edge down.

First thing you need is a puck. You want something light and stiff. The best puck is a 6"-8" styrofoam hemisphere (you can get them from a craft store). But assuming you don't have one of those, paper/plastic bowls are good and paper/styrofoam cups and empty soda cans work. Balloons work, although they're so easy, you lose some of the challenge and they tend to pop.

Next get a playing area that's flat, level and at least 10 yards long. Put the puck in the middle and a player on either side. The idea is to knock the puck with your yo across the other person's line (doing loops works the best). You get one point for each time you get it over.

You start with a face off, like regular hockey, "1, 2, 3, Go!" and you're off. Play to a score (11 is a good number) . After each point you start back at the middle with a face off.

Rule: you can't touch the puck with any part of your body and it can't touch you. If it does the other player gets a free shot from the point where the touch happened. The game resumes after the player's yo hit's the puck. In fact one strategy is to try and hit the other player with the puck so you can get the free shot.

And if you ace someone with your yo, it's a foul and they get a foul shot. A foul shot is a free shot from where the foul happened and then the game resumes with a stand off from where the puck ends up. But don't go foul-crazy, every time a yo touches someone it shouldn't be a foul. Fouls are when someone hits you badly or on purpose.

If the yos get tangled. The game immediately stops. Grab them as fast as you can to keep the knot from getting bad and untangle. Then each player gets to wind up and there's a face off from where the puck lays.

If your yo dies while the game is going on, tough luck. Wind it up real fast, the other person doesn't have to stop.

A variation of the game is playing it "Quick Draw". Quick draw is the same but you play in an area so small it only takes one hit to get it across the other person's line. So effectively it's a matter of who can hit the puck faster in the face off.

It's easiest to play hockey one on one, but if you want to play with more people you have to make sure that only one person from each team is trying to hit the puck at any time. The two ways to do this are to set up a hit rotation or set up zones.

With hit rotation when one player gets a hit the next player on the rotation has to take the next hit. When they get a hit it goes to the next player on the team and so on. So if your team was you, Alice, and the Mad Hatter and you were playing me and the Cheshire Cat the game would go like this: You and I start in the face off. You get the first

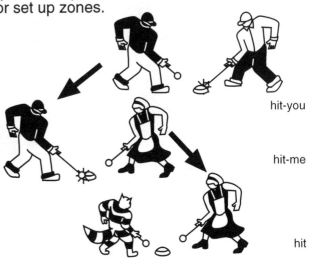

hit-you

hit-me

hit

hit, so Alice would have to get the next hit for your team. So it would be me and Alice going at it. Then I hit it so the Cheshire Cat goes at it with Alice. If the Cat hits it, I'll go back in. If Alice hits it, the Mad Hatter's in. You get the idea.

The other way is to set up zones. Basically you segment off the playing area into as many pieces as you have people on each team. Then one player from each team gets a section and when the puck moves into that section the two players from each team are the ones who go at it.

One person throws something in the air and the other person hits it. Not complicated. Usually soda cans or 16oz. plastic bottles are the easiest thing to use since they seem to be everywhere. One person throws it up to within range of the other person's yo and with a nice arc when they yell, "Pull". (that comes from real skeet shooting) If you want to keep score you can, but really it's just a challenge thing.

There is no culture in history where the warriors didn't decorate themselves and their weapons. Everything from paint and dye to bones and feathers. Since attaching bones and feathers to your yo tends to mess up the balance, it's best to stick with paint and stickers.

A good rule is to never get anything in your string gap. Keep all paint and especially sticker on the outsides.

A few hints:

1) Stickers are flat. If the sides of your yo are curved, they won't lie smooth. Usually yos have a flat section in the middle of curved sides so keep your stickers there. And feel free to cut up and trim stickers.

2) If you're on a team, one side should be your team logo and the other side should be your own designs.

3) Two words: Paint pens

4) If you have removable side panels take them off before you decorate them.

5) Radial designs can look really cool spinning.

6) Best technique for painting is to cover your yo with masking tape (flat and smooth) draw the design on it, then cut out the design with an exact-o knife (kids, have your parents do this). Give it a quick shot of spray paint (just little spritzes at a time. If it drips you're using too much), let it dry and then remove the tape.

7) It's better to buy the color yo you want than paint it on later.

8) Strings glow under black light if you soak them in whitening detergents with "brighteners".

9) Fabric dye and markers work on string.

(a few optical illusion patterns)

≈ 134 ≈

I never say that I "invented" a trick. There are two reasons: First is the belief that tricks are like spirits, they exist on their own. We don't make them, they just fly in, possess our yo for a few seconds and then fly on.

The less spiritual reason is that very often someone, somewhere, at sometime has done the trick before you. The Old Masters have done things with a yo that you can't imagine. The theories in this book are based on math that was first done somewhere in Asia Minor many thousands of years ago and the physics was discovered by Newton hundreds of years ago (quantum theory was coughed up by Einstein and his gang at the beginning of the twentieth century). That's why when someone asks me if I invented that trick I say, "Well... no one taught it to me." I never claim to have created a trick. It's a matter of respect for the spirits and the Old Masters.

But that aside, coming up with tricks, meeting new spirits, is great fun and is often how we learn a lot of our tricks. There are a few ways that this usually occurs. The first is when these things just happen. You miss one trick but it turns into another one, a random idea runs into you, a spirit walks up and introduces itself, you think "that was cool, but what if I..." These are all great ways and where a lot of great tricks are born. When it happens, do it again without thinking about it. Then think about it. Unconscious layers of your memory will remember these moves, then once they get it down, try to have your conscious memory remember. Or grab a friend and have them watch you. Use their conscious memory.

Another way to come up with tricks is hybriding. Hybriding a trick is taking part of one trick and attaching another part of another trick. Anytime you end up in a hold that is in another trick, you can skip over to that trick at that point. For example in Plan 9 and Splitting the Atom you have Fs.FYTF(14) holds. To hybrid these 2 you could start a Plan 9 and then when you got to that point, jump track and pick up a Splitting the Atom at the same hold.

Plan 9: Front Top Single Mount-Bs.YF(3), Throw Pluck-Bs.YFT(8), Throw Hop(Forward)-Bs.FTYT(14), Forward Free Lap-Bs.YFT(8), Free Morph (Backward)-Fs.FYTF(11), Backward Tumble-Bs.YFYTF, Throw Drop-Bs.YFYF(16), Unravel

Splitting the Atom: Back Bottom Split Mount-Fs.FYT(6), Free Underscoop-Fs.FYTF(11), Backward Tumble-Bs.YFYTF, Forward Roll, Drop Throw-Bs.YFYF(16), Forward Tumble-Fs.FYF(5), Unravle, Loop

Similar to hybriding is varying. A variation is a trick that is done differently. Doing a trick from the opposite side is an uncomplicated variation. Throwing zero moves into the middle of a trick is an easy way to get a variation. And get creative; think backwards, sideways, inverted, deviated...

Another way to come across new tricks is to play chemist and synthesize them with Quantum Yo Theory. You'll notice in the Holds section that there is a listing of each move you can do to each hold and what you end up with. This is a link by link write up of any chain you can go with. In fact on the next page is the whole thing drawn up as a subway map. You can chart where you're going and where you've been and use that to figure out new paths... and boldly go where you've never gone before.

Again, these write ups don't include holds with more than 5 segs or mutations. Both are usually more than you want to deal with, but as Splitting the Atom and Oliver Twist showed us, you can move in and out of these realms with some pretty cool results. And as the section on Untranscribables and the entire history of yoyology until now shows us, there's plenty to do with a yo beyond the range of trigonometry and QYT.

It's always good to meet new players. They're a great source for new whole tricks and they're a great source of new ideas. Your arsenal of tricks will blend with your friends as you're around each other and learn each other's moves. But then one day some out of towner rolls through and you trade tricks and he's doing things you've never thought of and you're doing things that he's never thought of. It's like Marco Polo, he's in Italy living on lamb chops and ceasar salad, then he goes to China and comes back with noodles, sweet and sour sauce, lo mein, and whatever else. It's not only a bunch of new recipes, but new ideas and new thing to add to old recipes. Foreign travelers are haunted by foreign spirits.

Map of the QYT Subway

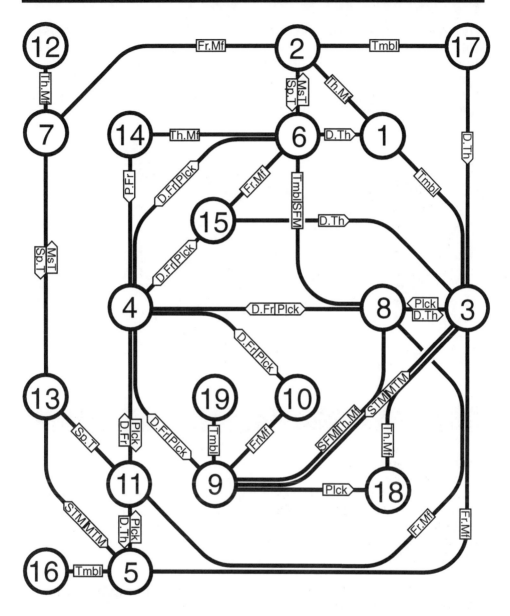

Tmbl-Tumble
Fr.Mf-Free Morph
Th.Mf-Throw Morph
Sp.T-Split Tumble
Ms.T-Miss Tumble
SFM-Split Free Morph

STM-Split Throw Morph
MTM-Miss Throw Morph
D.Fr-Free Finger Drop
D.Th-Throw Finger Drop
Plck-Throw Pluck (Free out of 4)

Dead Spin

A dead spin, apart from being an oxymoron (ask your local dictionary, kids), is a technique for teaching, learning and working out tricks. Real simple: You get a friend to hold your yo in line while you slowly work through what you're working on (by the side, being careful not to cover the string gap). This way you can keep the plane and stability well beyond the time that the spin would run down.

Swivels

Another thing I've seen people do is splicing fishing swivels into the top of their strings so they don't have to worry about their string getting loose or tight. This is worth while if you're going for a looping record or if all you do is loop tricks. The problem for the rest of us is that the ability to change the tightness of the string is a good thing for when you change from one kind of trick to another. But it's something to keep in mind.

If you do splice a swivel into your string do it up near your hand so it doesn't interfere with the yo.

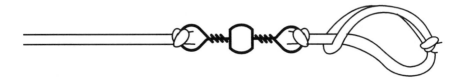

Extromanual yoing is involving other things besides your hands in your tricks. It's a great way to throw a little variety into your throwing.

Grinders- Grind is a move that inherently involves something else. I mentioned briefly in its write up that the best things were balance runs and loud stuff. The gyroscopic stability that keeps a plane will also keep your yo upright when you lay it out on to stuff. Thus making it easier to balance a spinning yo on something really narrow, like the back of a chair.

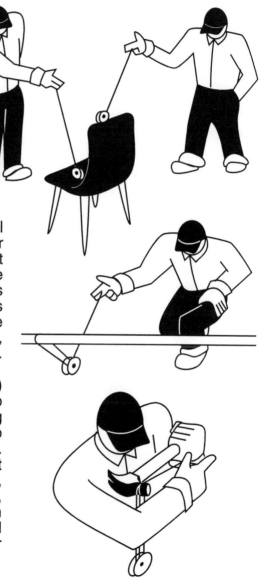

The other thing to remember is that hollow, stiff objects usually make a good racket. Fiberglass chair seats and thin wooden boxes are the best.

One of my favorite extromanual moves is throwing moves over a rail. Any firm bar at the right height, with the right clearance will do. Over and under mounts work great. If you have 2 bars above each other (like the cross supports of a bar stool), you can go between them.

Prosthetics are extra (fake) body parts or extensions. In yo terms this means using something else in addition to or instead of your free hand. Same moves and tricks but your 3 points are throwhand, yo, and peg in a wall, chair arm, police baton, foot, whatever. In fact you can get crazy and create prosthetics. Use your imagination.

Index

Keep up with the on-going quest for the lost books of The Yonomicon online at

www.yonomicon.com

Also check **www.yoyoing.com** and **www.ayya.pd.net**

≈ end ≈